Message from an Unknown Chinese Mother

Message from an Unknown Chinese Mother

STORIES OF LOSS AND LOVE

XINRAN

Translated from Chinese by Nicky Harman

Chatto & Windus

LONDON

Published by Chatto & Windus 2010

2 4 6 8 10 9 7 5 3 1

First published in Great Britain in 2010 by
Chatto & Windus
Random House, 20 Vauxhall Bridge Road,
London SW1V 2SA
www.rbooks.co.uk

Addresses for companies within The Random House Group Limited can be found at:
www.randomhouse.co.uk/offices.htm

The Random House Group Limited Reg. No. 954009

A CIP catalogue record for this book
is available from the British Library

Hardback ISBN 9780701184025
Trade Paperback ISBN 9780701184032

The Random House Group Limited supports The Forest Stewardship
Council (FSC), the leading international forest certification organisation. All our titles
that are printed on Greenpeace approved FSC certified paper carry the FSC logo. Our
paper procurement policy can be found at www.rbooks.co.uk/environment

Mixed Sources
Product group from well-managed
forests and other controlled sources
www.fsc.org Cert no. TT-COC-2139
© 1996 Forest Stewardship Council
FSC

Typeset in Sabon by Palimpsest Book Production Ltd
Grangemouth, Stirlingshire

Printed and bound in Great Britain by
CPI Mackays, Chatham ME5 8TD

A Book for Chinese Adoptees –

and for MBLers

Translator's Note

The stories in this book are immensely powerful, and in one way that made them harder to translate. Clearly, the translation required emotional sensitivity. When mothers talked about their lost daughters, it was especially important to choose the words which struck the right 'note'; the language had to be convincing to the reader – neither too emotional nor too understated. Above all, these women's words had to sound as natural to the reader as they did to Xinran when she listened to the speaker. But Chinese is a very different language from English, and sometimes translating too literally doesn't convey the emotions behind the words. Then there are words for which there is only one obvious translation which, however, turns out to have a meaning significantly different from the original Chinese. In *Message from an Unknown Chinese Mother*, for instance, 'roots', doesn't mean a birthplace or community to which one returns, as it does in the West. To Chinese villagers, 'roots' are a person – the son who has the sacred duty to honour the ancestors and, in so doing, maintain the family 'line'. In addition, some of the words these people use – especially in those stories which have a rural background – described things I had never seen or heard of, and which didn't appear in dictionaries. What was the 'candle bag' in which a new-born baby was wrapped, for instance? When I was really stumped, Xinran was a model author, always willing to answer my questions and as keen for me to get it right as I was myself.

There were also customs which I knew about but which required an extra word of explanation for the reader, the Birth Month, for instance. A narrative of this kind is filled with references to customs and beliefs, the kind so strongly held and so deeply rooted in the community that they drive people to extreme actions. Xinran has interpreted and explained these for the reader but, as the translator, I still had to tread carefully.

One of the joys of translation is a sense of privilege: we're lucky people, because we have a window into another world. The translator is a kind of bridge-builder between two languages and cultures. I hope that through my translation, I've helped to make the experiences of the women and men who 'speak' in this book more real to its readers, whoever or wherever they may be.

Nicky Harman

Contents

Background Note

By the end of 2007, the number of Chinese orphans adopted world-wide had reached 120,000. These children had gone to twenty-seven countries – and almost all were girls. Most Chinese find the adoption figures almost incredible, just as they find it hard to believe that Chinese children have found mothers and homes in so many countries. Why does China have so many orphaned girls? Most Chinese would say that it is because there is something inherently wrong with tradit-ional culture; in other words, old customs are rooted in ignorance. Westerners, on the other hand, believe that the one-child policy is to blame. I began to gather information for myself when, in 1989, I started presenting *Words on the Night Breeze*, a programme for women on Nanjing Radio; as this job took me all over China doing interviews, I came across women who had been forced to abandon their babies. Personally, I feel there are three main reasons why. Firstly, female babies have been abandoned in farming cultures of the East since ancient times; secondly, a combination of sexual ignorance, which remains rife, and the economic boom; and lastly, there is the one-child policy.

In developing countries, with their communities which rely on prim-itive methods of farming, or on hunting, gathering and fishing, hard manual labour is necessary for survival; so a preference for boys is inevitable. Males have an indisputable physical advantage over females when it comes to labouring, carrying goods, hunting, defence and so on.

Another factor that cannot be ignored in China is an ancient system of land distribution that still persists today. It began with the Xia dynasty (approx. 2070 BC to 1600 BC) and found its most complete form in the Well Field System of the Zhou dynasty (1045 BC to 256 BC), and the Equal Field System set up around AD 485 by the Northern Wei rulers.* What these had in common with the present system is the principle of allocating fields based on the number of household members. Discrimination in favour of men became, therefore, an immutable law.† In AD 485 a list was drawn up of households, and then land was allocated based on the number of permanent household members. Land was divided into two kinds: arable fields, for growing grain, and mulberry tree land, for feeding the silkworms. Every male aged fifteen years or more received 40 *mu*‡ of arable land, while females received 20 *mu*, and slaves and servants could also be allocated land. This land reverted to the government on death.

As for 'mulberry tree' land, males received 20 *mu*, and this became their property – they could buy and sell it and it did not need to be handed back to the government. During the Tang dynasty, AD 618–907, it was clearly stipulated that females were not normally to be given their own land. And so dynasties have come and gone through Chinese history, but the ways in which land is apportioned has never really changed, and the basic inequality between men and women has become a deeply entrenched tradition. In the villages, boy children not only carried on the family line and inherited the clan name, they were also the source of the family property and the creator of its wealth.

Article 22 of the 'Population and Family Planning Law of the People's Republic of China' promulgated on 29 December 2001 says: 'Discrimination against and mistreatment of women who give birth to female children or who suffer from infertility is prohibited. Discrimination against, or mistreatment and abandonment of female infants is prohibited.' However, a 'good woman' must give birth to a boy – every married village woman knows this. It is both her god-given duty and her parents-in-law's most fervent hope. So in some

---

* The system originated in China in AD 485 by order of Emperor Xiaowendi of the Northern Wei dynasty (AD 386–534/535). (*Trans.*)

† Because girls moved to other families on marriage, they would not be given land while still living with their birth families. (*Trans.*)

‡ In modern China, one *mu* is equal to 1/6 acre or 1/16 hectare. In ancient China, however, the size of a *mu* varied according to the historical period and also to the type of land. (*Trans.*)

poorer villages, if the first child is a girl, the unfortunate child is abandoned or even smothered at birth. Where birth control is not properly
understood, abandoning infants is just another law of nature which
has operated from time immemorial. If the extra infant the family
could not bring up was a boy, he would often be adopted by another
family or sold. For a girl, death was almost inevitable.

China's one-child-per-family policy was drawn up at the Second
National Symposium on Population held in the city of Chengdu,
Sichuan province, on 11–14 December 1979. The then Vice-Premier Chen
Muhua (who also happened to be the first woman premier in China's
history) convinced delegates in the closing debate that limiting couples
to one child could slow the rapid rate of population growth in China.
That was the start of the 'population revolution' which remains the
subject of fierce debate to this day. The renowned Chinese specialist
in population studies, Professor Ma Yanchu,* had warned in the early

---

* The economist Ma Yanchu (1882–1992) entered Beiyang University in Tianjin in 1901 to study
mining and metallurgy; after a masters in economics at Yale University, and a doctorate at
Columbia University, he returned to China in 1915, and worked first in the Ministry of Finance of
Yuan Shikai's republican 'Beiyang Government' and later as professor of economics at Peking
University. In August 1949, he became head of Zhejiang University and held a number of government positions. He began to focus his research on the problem of the rapid expansion of China's
population growth in the early 1950s, publishing New Theory of Population. Ma stressed the
need to accumulate capital, develop science and technology, improve labour productivity, standards of living and educational levels, and increase supplies of industrial raw materials;
concluding that there was an urgent need to control population numbers, he made three main
points: (1) Only if population numbers were controlled could consumption be brought down,
allowing capital accumulation. (2) To build socialism, it was necessary to increase labour productivity, to develop heavy industry and to electrify and mechanise agriculture. (3) There was a
conflict between agriculture and industrial raw materials; population pressure on food resources
meant that there was little land on which to cultivate cotton, silkworms, soya beans, peanuts
and other cash crops. 'For food reasons alone, the population must be controlled', he wrote, and
this should be done without delay. Ma raised the population problem with Mao Zedong on
many occasions. Mao Zedong disagreed: 'Can we plan the production of people? Can we subject
them to studies and experiments?' A nationwide campaign was launched to criticise 'Ma Yanchu's
reactionary thinking'. But Ma stood firm, and although he was by then getting on in years, he
declared publicly: 'For the sake of my country and the truth, I will continue to uphold my population theory, no matter what. I do not fear being attacked or isolated, nor do I fear hardship,
dismissal, imprisonment, even death itself.' On 3 January 1960, he was forced to resign from his
position as head of Peking University, and soon afterwards was relieved of his duties on the
Standing Committee of the People's Congress. He was forbidden to publish, speak publicly, give
interviews to reporters, or receive overseas visitors even if they were friends. For his misdeeds,
he was also placed under house arrest.
  After the demise of the Gang of Four, Ma Yanchu was reappointed head of Peking
University. He died shortly before his 100th birthday, on 14 May 1982.

1950s that the country's population was growing too fast; at his suggestion, the government carried out China's first population survey in the early part of 1953. The results were published on 1 November of that year: at midnight on 1 June 1953, the Chinese population stood at 600 million. In just four years since the establishment of the People's Republic of China in 1949, the population had grown by 100 million. In his comparative study, *New Theory of Population* (1957) Professor Ma wrote that in the years 1953–57 the population may actually have exceeded the 20 per cent annual increase found in the 1953 survey. In his view, the slow growth of manufacturing technology together with a surge in population with its attendant social conflicts meant that as the global economy and civilisation developed, China would lag behind. Ma's ideas were diametrically opposed to Mao's, which were that the population and the economy should grow in parallel. As a result, Ma was persecuted during the Cultural Revolution.

But history proved Ma right: the population continued to grow – from 700 million in 1966 to 1.2 billion in 1979 – while education and the economy lagged far behind that of the developed world. Even today, most city-dwellers over the age of forty-five will remember the treasured ration coupons for oil, meat, grain and cloth. One year, I remember queuing from five o'clock in the morning until twelve noon in the snow and freezing temperatures to buy a quarter kilo of pork for my teacher. This was the ration for the entire family for their Chinese New Year dinner! In the countryside, the population continued to grow. The increasing narrowness of roads between the fields was mute proof of the struggles to wrest food from every tiny scrap of land. To put it bluntly, the economy was stagnating and the imposition of a population control policy offered a tiny respite in the daily struggle for survival for a people who had suffered a century of war and political upheavals, and battled daily with poverty.

Millions of families, however, continued to believe that it was their god-given duty to produce a male heir to carry on the family line; in fact it was a sin not to do so. As the 'family planning era' really got under way in the 1980s, these people paid a heavy price. Whole families were ruined, homes destroyed and people died at the hands of village cadres who carried out family planning policies crudely and violently. It was illiterate peasant families who fought the local government most bitterly for the chance to have a baby boy.

There is a Chinese saying I've quoted before that 'the heavens are high and the emperor far away', meaning that the further one goes from the centre of government, the more likely it is that local rules will prevail over edicts from the capital. With an area of 9,600,000 km², China is a vast country and there are areas where the one-child policy has never been effectively implemented. In the most remote mountain areas in the west of China only lip service is paid to it. In 2006, when I was doing interviews for my book, *China Witness*, in the region bounded by the Yellow River and the Yangtze River, I came across many families with five or more children in mountain villages in the west (there were exemptions for ethnic minority groups); even in the east of China, poor peasant families with three or more children were common. Not all twenty-somethings in China are only children; there are also many with hordes of brothers and sisters.

In contrast, in eastern China's urban areas, enforcement was and is draconian.* Almost everyone lived within the state-planned economy up until the beginning of the 1990s. So having more than one child meant losing your job, your home (which was allocated by your employer), your entitlement to food and clothing rations, your child's entitlement to schooling and medical care, and even your chance of finding other work, as no one would dare employ you. Just because you had had one 'extra' child, you and your family would forfeit absolutely everything. Amongst educated people, there were very few indeed who were prepared to run the risk of ruining their prospects in this way. However, that did not stop them employing every possible means from modern medical technology to traditional Chinese herbal remedies to ensure the birth of a boy. I think this goes some way to explaining the gender imbalance in some areas of China.

In the many years I have spent interviewing people in the course of my work, I have discovered yet another simple but very important reason why babies are abandoned: the combination of sexual ignorance and sexual freedom among young people.

Looking back at the first decade of the economic reforms, it is

---

* However, in July 2009 the Shanghai authorities publicly announced an official relaxation (already in practice in the city over the last few years) in the one-child policy. Concerned about the balance of population – as a result of a dwindling birthrate among the educated classes and an ageing population – they have begun to encourage the births of second children in certain sectors of the population.

clear that 1992 marked a turning-point for China's urban population. Up until that time, educated city-dwellers had been onlookers. Many even dismissed the reforms as yet another political movement. They looked down on migrants from the countryside who laboured furiously to lift themselves out of absolute poverty; and they positively despised those former jobless vagrants who now prospered as small stall-holders in cities and towns. In the 1980s, '10,000 yuan-a-year family' was just another name for uneducated people who had made money through taking risks. The educated were more cautious. It took a decade for them to wake up to the fact that, if they wanted to keep up, they must take their courage in both hands and grab the opportunities offered by the reforms. A great wave of young people soon swamped colleges and universities. Business became fashionable, and so did everything Western. And as far as young students went, the reforms appeared to find their most dramatic expression in 'Westernised' relations between the sexes – there was a sudden surge in the number of young people sleeping together without getting married.

A friend of mine in China once lamented to me in a phone call that she no longer knew what social rules operated and what morality meant. 'In our day,' she said, 'no one would dare even to have a private chat with a member of the opposite sex. Our parents would not kiss or embrace each other in front of the children! But now, my nineteen-year-old daughter changes her boyfriend every couple of months, and often stays out all night. She calls it sexual freedom and running her own life! I don't know any more, are there any social standards left?'

I am not going to discuss here what social standards we ought to have. Judging the whole world by the same set of standards is ignorant and authoritarian. What I do want to talk about is those young people, my friend's daughter's generation, who grew up in the 1990s. They went from living in a society where traditional moral standards still prevailed, straight to adopting Westernised sexual mores. The problem was that many of them had had virtually no sex education or guidance: they lived a 'sexless' existence within the family, at school and in society. A combination of factors – sexual ignorance, the absence of sexual health programmes, and hypocritical attitudes to sexuality among the older generation – meant that when the young were

suddenly exposed to Westernised sexual liberation and the new hedo-
nism, the consequences were disastrous. Many young women knew
nothing of contraception, or even how babies were made. The abortion business became a great way to make quick money, and
advertisements for such services were plastered all over the outskirts
of cities. Almost none of those students who now found themselves
pregnant kept their babies. Chinese families fought over the boys, but
the girl babies inevitably ended up in orphanages. This is probably
one of the reasons for the dramatic increase in numbers of girl babies
in Chinese orphanages from 1990 onward, and also for the 1992 government policy permitting international adoption.*

Of course, there are also other reasons why newborn infants are
abandoned, and they are even more distressing and horrific. For
instance, a soothsayer might predict that 'it will spare the family
trouble in the future'; and there are also folk beliefs that killing an
infant will 'avert natural catastrophes'. Among many peoples, there
are persistent beliefs about abandoning babies which have been handed
down by the elders of the community.

In this book, you will read tragic stories of what has traditionally
happened to abandoned girl babies, and what continues to happen.
The tools for enforcing these traditions have been forged from a need
to survive, and honed by mothers over centuries – and yet the victims
are themselves women and girls. In 2004 I set up a charity in the UK
called The Mothers' Bridge of Love (MBL). It has three main aims: to
provide cultural resources for Chinese children living all over the world;
to help those children who had been adopted into Western families,
and so had a dual cultural heritage; and, especially, to provide help for
disabled children who languished forgotten in Chinese orphanages.

---

* In my work, as well as investigating what the cultural needs of Chinese adopted children
were, I also learned about the adoption laws. The Adoption Law of the People's Republic of
China was passed at the 23rd Meeting of the Standing Committee of the Seventh National
People's Congress on 29 December 1991 and came into force on 1 April 1992. It was amended
at the 5th Meeting of the Standing Committee of the Ninth National People's Congress, on
4 November 1998. Then in 2005, China signed up to the Hague Convention of 29 May 1993
on Protection of Children and Co-operation in Respect of Intercountry Adoption (Hague
Adoption Convention). See Appendix B.

Foreword: A Book Written for Adopted Daughters

IT TOOK a long time for me to summon the courage to relive certain of the memories and personal experiences of my life as a reporter in China. In *The Good Women of China* I wrote about those brave women who had told me their stories when I worked as a radio presenter. But there were some stories I could not yet bring myself to tell. They were too painful and too close to home. I am not a particularly courageous woman; I am just a woman who longs to feel a mother's embrace and that lifelong bond of love and dependence between mother and daughter. Little by little, that longing seeped through me until it began to dominate my thoughts day and night. Reawakening those memories threatened to reopen old wounds: I would miss my own mother more than ever, and would feel even more bitter that I could never have that kind of love.

At a talk I gave at the International Book Fair in Melbourne, Australia, in 2002, someone asked me: 'Xinran, what is your dream?'

I said: 'To be a daughter.'

There was uproar from the audience of several hundred people. 'But you were born, so you must be someone's daughter!'

'In a biological sense, yes,' I responded. 'But I was born into a traditional culture, I experienced brutal political upheavals as a child, and my mother and I lived in times which did not consider bonds of family affection important. The result is there's not a single occasion I can remember when my mother said she loved me, or even hugged me.'

After the meeting, I found a line of silver-haired women standing waiting for me by the car which was to take me back to my hotel. They were there, they said, to give me a mother's embrace. One by one they came up to me, put their arms around me, and kissed my forehead . . .

I could not help myself, tears poured down my face. In my heart, I cried: 'I'm grateful for their genuine affection, but how I wish my own mother could have held me like this. I miss my mother's love so much!' And that is the reason why I was afraid to go back to memories which cost me so many tears at the time and to revisit the pain of women who had abandoned their daughters. It was even more difficult to face the question asked by Chinese girls adopted into foreign cultures: 'Xinran, do you know why my Chinese mother didn't want me?'

My books have been published and translated into more than thirty languages and, as a result, I have received photographs, tapes and videos from adopting families and adopted Chinese girls from all over the world. Their letters, like the two which follow (and the others on pp.175–77 and pp. 183–86), offered me comfort, and it is with their encouragement that I have finally written down here the stories of Chinese women who were forced to abandon their babies . . .

Dear Xinran

I am the (adoptive) mother of two beautiful daughters of China. My daughters are now 11 and 9. They both are very happy in our family and much loved. They also will never forget they have a birth family in China. They love their birth mothers and both of them, like you, would very much like to see their birth mother's face and hear her words. Please write your book. In this way they will know the heart of their birth mothers. Though we have told them we will look for their birth mothers if they desire to find them, we have also told them such a search may not be successful. The message you send from birth mothers may be all they ever have of their Chinese family.

One thing you can tell the Chinese birth mothers is that their daughters have not forgotten them. In our family their birth mothers are honored. My daughters and I study Pu Tong Hua. We have already returned to China 2 times with our daughters. They love the land of their birth, as their Father and I do. We are proud to be an American Chinese family.

Please send our love, gratitude, and honor to their Chinese Mothers.

Thank you,

The Macechko Family,

(USA)

Dear Xinran,

So lovely to hear from you. I know just what you mean about how it takes days for your 'head' to arrive back after your body. Flying around the world is such an odd experience in that way.

Please, please, please do write Messages from Chinese Mums. *You have to write it for all those girls. Mei and Xue even now ask why their 'tummy mummy' couldn't look after them. I have to say, I don't know. Because I do not know. I can't lie. I can only guess – maybe poverty, maybe post natal depression, maybe rape, maybe the fact that they are girls, maybe she was a teenager? I can only guess at the pain. I save all books and newspaper clippings of China, so that when the girls are big, they can read what life was like and try and understand – maybe understand what their birth mother experienced. But, if you wrote some stories of the Chinese mothers, it would be more clearly explained.*

I couldn't read the Good Women of China *because I found it too painful. I cried and cried and cried. Each woman, I thought of as Mei and Xue's mother – and what she had to bear and what loss for her to leave her babies. Some day all those adopted girls have to understand that their mothers gave them up – (HOPE-FULLY) not because she didn't love them, but because life was too hard and too painful to bear. They must understand this fully. This is the only way to heal the pain for them of being rejected in that way.*

Mei and Xue have bought such joy to our lives. Barry and I are complete with them and our family is a tight beautiful bond. But, I am aware that somewhere there is a mother (if she is alive) who has a deep pain about her girls. I want her to know that the girls are alive and happy and for her not to worry. But, I also know that life is very complex and a well-intentioned westerner can cause many problems easily.

I understand fully about MBL. It is very important. The link between all those girls and their mothers. The link between women of the world is very important. For some, your books are just stories, but for many of us, they are much more than that. Someday Mei and Xue will read your books and understand a little about their birth mum's life and those of their birth grandmothers. We can only thank you for that.

. . .

With big hugs Xinran (Mei and Xue send them also). They are fascinated by you – Xue is very literary and loves the idea that you write books. She had me read out your email (I read out bits). Both girls sense some link with you. It is very interesting. Do come back and see us and come and stay when you are next over.

With love, Ros
(New Zealand)

*

I received so many letters, I was almost swamped by them. The things that they said often come back to me, and make me wonder: if I were an adopted daughter myself, how would I cope? Where would I find answers to the questions which such a strange start in life must throw up?

In April 2007, I went back to China and tried once more to confront my mother. I wanted to unburden myself of memories stored in the deepest, darkest recesses of my soul; I wanted to tell her what had happened to me, her daughter, during the Cultural Revolution when she was not with me. I wanted her to understand the nightmarish torments I went through, and which still haunt me. For her to know how much I missed her and still long for her, my mother. But, just as on countless previous occasions, I could not get a word out. I just sat silently in front of her, in floods of tears. But this time, something was different: sitting there in silence I began to understand how those adopted daughters long to understand their birth mothers and to tell them how much they love them. I realised that in a small way I was one of them. That day I decided that, no matter how painful it was, I would write down the stories I had stored up for so long. I could share my thoughts and feelings about mothers and about life with adopted daughters and, in this way, thank the adoptive mothers for their love for their Chinese daughters.

As the memories gradually began to emerge and I took up my pen to write, other fears assailed me: should I write it as documentary evidence, or should I fictionalise it? What should I put in, what should I leave out? What image of their birth mother would it give to adopted children? Should I embellish the facts or leave them unadorned? Should I let my choice of those facts be dictated by my emotions? It took me nearly ten months of wrestling with these doubts before I eventually came up with my own answers. This book was to be an honest record of mothers' lives, a gift of mother–daughter love which I, a daughter, could share with other daughters, a message from an unknown Chinese mother to her daughter, wherever she may be.

I started writing this book on 2 February 2008, in a little house by the sea in Blues Point Road, Sydney, Australia. Strangely, my labours were accompanied by a fortnight of the violent storms which a southern hemisphere summer sometimes brings. Did the Almighty know the emotional turmoil I was feeling, my terror of putting those memories down on paper? Was my resolve being strengthened in dramatic fashion?

February the 7th was the Chinese New Year, or Spring Festival, and the Australian media reported on the tens of thousands of Chinese who joined in the cultural festivities. Among them were over a hundred families who had adopted Chinese children. As I watched these girls dressed in Chinese costumes asking their Australian parents in English what the Spring Festival was, I had very mixed feelings. Were these girls really China's daughters? Yes, I think they were. As the ancients said: when oranges from the south were transplanted to the north, they were still oranges, even if they tasted a bit different. I believe that even though these girls have been brought up in a foreign land and a foreign culture, the blood of their Chinese mothers still runs in their veins.

But what do their birth mothers feel? Does the unknown Chinese mother feel joy or sorrow at knowing that her beloved daughter is now happy in another mother's arms? I did not actually give birth to a daughter, nor am I the mother of an adopted daughter, but I weep every time I try to imagine how they feel. And once I lost a little girl who was like a daughter to me, so I know something of what they feel. There is an emptiness which can never be filled, there is an ache felt by the broken-hearted birth mother, by the adoptive family in the West and by the daughter who will spend the rest of her life in a dual embrace – because the life she lives is a product of great joy but also of great sorrow.

The names of people and places have all been changed in this book, in order to protect the privacy of the birth mothers. Their stories, however, are all true.

1

The First Mother I Met Who
Had Lost Her Daughter

*'My name is Waiter – not "waiter" in the sense of someone who
waits at tables in a restaurant, but meaning someone who waits
for a future which will never come.'*

WHEN I said farewell to China and made my way to England
in the summer of 1997, I travelled with the emotional
baggage of forty difficult years in China – and all my material
possessions stuffed into a single suitcase. I was going to a country
I knew nothing about, and I was bringing almost nothing into
my new life. I could pick and choose only a few bits of 'home'
to take with me, and these could not exceed the permitted 25
kilos.

Apart from day-to-day necessities, of which I never had
many, I had other possessions I was particularly attached to
and which I had accumulated over the twenty adult years before
my departure: especially books, stones and music tapes. All of
these things had made me what I am, both as a woman and a
mother; and the story of 'the first mother' has to start with my
own journey . . .

My love of books began when the flames of the Cultural
Revolution destroyed a hitherto happy childhood. I was being
reduced to tears by bullies on a daily basis, and so one of my
language teachers took pity on me and hid me in a back room

filled with books which he had saved from the Red Guards' bonfires. In this cubbyhole (as I have described in *The Good Women of China*), its window pasted over with newspaper, I began to read by the light let in through a small hole. The first great work of literature which was to offer me an escape from my misery was a Chinese translation of Victor Hugo's *Les Misérables*; I was surprised, as I glanced down the first page, and read about the humiliations suffered by little Cosette as she slaved away in that sordid bar, to realise that there were people in the world very much worse off than me.

The battles in *Les Misérables*, and the hardships and bloody struggles that filled the lives of its protagonists, restored a sense of balance to me in those dark days. I was not the only lonely, suffering child; I was living in the real world, and it was not all bad. At least I was not living hand-to-mouth, with a war raging around me, as they were. At least I had enough to eat, and I had books.

I began to spend most of my money on history books, biographies, books on world culture, and translations of classics, until they filled my house. Every new volume would give me a supreme sense of satisfaction, as well as new knowledge, and I read until far into the night. When I emigrated, I not only had to strike root in a strange country and 'grow up' all over again. I also had to go through the excruciating process of parting with my beloved book collection, which by then totalled several thousand volumes. More than 2,000 went to the Baixia Children's Palace in Nanjing, where I set up a little library for the parents who brought their children every weekend to study art and other skills. Another 2,000 or so I gave to the wives of volunteer soldiers from poor areas, many of whom could not read or write, so that they could set up an Adult Education Library. Nearly 2,000 illustrated books, on China, history and life in other countries, as well as quantities of children's books, went to migrant worker women who lived clustered on the city outskirts; their children were first-generation city folk but had never taken part in any cultural activities. I hoped that my books could help to educate the parents of the future.

That left 200 books which I definitely could not take to my

new home. I deposited them in a good friend's office, where they told the world how cultured she was. Finally, a dozen or more books with which I really could not bear to part occupied one-third of my small suitcase.

My love of stones, and a curious collection which grew from a hobby into something much more important for me, came from a trip I made at the end of the 1980s. I had gone to a small mountain village near Yulin, in Shaanxi province, to interview a woman who was something of a local legend. She had a deeply lined face and rough hands with misshapen fingers, her skin was engrained with decades of dirt, and she reeked of smoke. Every now and then, she wiped the snot that ran from her nose, rubbing her fingers clean on her clothes. Looking at her, I found it almost impossible to believe her extraordinary tale. In the 1950s, when she was a girl, her parents returned from America to help with 'national reconstruction', but were arrested as spies when the government discovered a plot by overseas Chinese and the Taiwan-based enemy Guomindang. She was a teenager at the time, and the night before their arrest she was taken by a family friend into hiding in the poorest part of the Shanxi mountains.

At the start of the Cultural Revolution, it was arranged that she should marry one of the poorest of the local men – this protected her by putting her into the 'Red' camp. She had kept three photographs as a testament to her story: one showed a happy girl in a dress hugging her parents; in another she was playing the piano, dressed in a white evening dress; and the third was of her parents, dressed in Western clothes and standing in front of their American home. The woman I was interviewing looked like any other peasant – there was no trace of her former wealthy, elegant life – although I could see a physical resemblance to her parents.

'However did you . . . did you . . . ?' I really did not know how to put my question.

'How did I cope? Is that what you're asking?' She wiped her nose again, and pointed unsmilingly to a stream which ran through a crack in the rock near her feet. She said: 'Choose a pebble and break it open. That will tell you!'

I picked out a pebble and cracked it open with a bigger stone, but could see no answer to my question inside.

'Why is a pebble round?' She was obviously annoyed that I was being so obtuse.

'It's been worn smooth by time and the water, hasn't it?' I answered hesitantly.

'What about inside? Does the water get inside it? That's where the woman is.' She threw this last comment at me, and walked off.

And then I understood: a woman was like a pebble worn smooth and round by water and time. Our outward appearance was changed by the fate meted out to us in our lives, but no water could alter the heart of the woman and her maternal instincts.

After that, I fell in love with pebbles; they seemed to symbolise my desire to fathom the true nature of Chinese women.

In my travels around the world, I could not carry heavy stones with me. After much agonising, I gave my beloved pebbles, collected during reporting trips, to friends. I do not know if they understood my feelings about the stories behind each one, and about the 'pebble' that I was becoming as I grew older. You have to understand why they are valuable to appreciate them. I did not know how far my journey would take me, or for how long. I just felt reassured that the pebbles I had left in my friends' hands would not wear away during our lifetime, and that no disasters would destroy them. I took only one pebble with me. It was one which had accompanied me for years in spirit and in my actual journeys around China; I had picked it up on the banks of the Yangtze River when some strange fate ordained that I should meet first a mother, then a daughter, whose stories you can read in Chapter 9 of this book.

The only 'fashionable' items which I had amongst my belongings were a few hundred music CDs and about a hundred old-style tape-recordings. DVDs were only just then becoming popular in China, and I could not afford them.

(I did not have many VCDs either, for what to me seemed a good reason, though no doubt others thought me ridiculous: watching VCDs was mainly associated in my mind with corrupt officials who groped the office secretaries by day, spent their evenings in the arms of escort girls in karaoke bars, slept with their lovers at weekends, and then went home to shout abuse at the wife for being dull. Whenever I thought about getting some VCDs, I felt a rush of loathing for those drunken creeps. Years of presenting radio shows for women, listening to tearful accusations from fatherless children, and frank confessions of husbands stolen away by other women, had taught me that one reason why these men callously deserted their families was the irresistible draw of karaoke. That dreamlike setting, that unforgettable smile, those heart-stopping lyrics, that whiff of fragrance from the singer standing next to them . . .)

But the music tapes were different and I found it really hard to part with them. They had been with me from the moment at the end of the 1980s when the mainstream media started to use popular music or Western classical music to accompany its broadcasts, through to the late 1990s, when China, rushing headlong into economic development, fell in love with Western culture. Deng Xiaoping forced open the creaking door which had sealed China off from the outside world for thousands of years and, as I saw it, the music that flooded in fed the parched souls of young Chinese people. At that time, no one had computers, and most people did not have television or telephones either. Long-distance communication was limited to the monotonous tones of government propaganda broadcasts. In 1980s China, the most 'advanced' culture was represented by Chinese songs and plays that dated back to the 1950s. Every Chinese man or woman over forty has a favourite song that never fails to move them. These rousing rhythms nourished their battered, repressed and impoverished spirits, and the lyrics promised love and affection to flesh which craved the forbidden fruit of sexual love.

When I read my listeners' letters, I found that a popular tune or the evocative lines of a song often replayed themselves in my head, and my response was to put on a song or some bars of a melody. Those old-style tapes for me became a repository of the spirit of those times.

I steeled myself to make my intrepid dash towards a totally unknown future in the West by taking with me only the music that I knew and loved and could not imagine life without: a Chinese CD of *Paradiesvogel* and two tapes, of Enya Brennan and Schumann.

Robert Schumann's *Träumerei* was the introductory music to the first programme I hosted on Nanjing Radio, *Words on the Night Breeze*. I never imagined that my words and the soft, dream-like notes of Schumann's piece would attract over a hundred letters every day, but I knew as the music began to play that I was going to be a plain-speaking presenter on a programme which I would make very much my own.

The Chinese CD of *Paradiesvogel* is a selection of the best of James Last's panpipe music,* and modern classics both Western and Chinese. I particularly like 'Edelweiss' and 'Moscow Suburbs Night', as well as others that the women who listened to my programme sometimes mentioned.

Enya† was first heard in China at the end of the 1980s, at a time when the Chinese media had just started live broadcasting for its main programmes. When I heard her voice during my routine work of listening to newly issued recordings, I remember how struck I was by those languorous sounds. The truth is that her singing not only brought tears to my eyes, but stirred up in my heart indescribable emotions – fleeting, dreamlike, yet frenzied and with the power to awaken me. And her glorious music took me on a voyage of exploration to every corner of the world which continues to this day.

*

When I first played Enya in my programme, I chose 'Evening Falls', 'Orinoco Flow' and 'Na Laetha Geal M'Óige' from her *Watermark* album as background music in response to listeners'

---

* Panpipes are an ancient Chinese instrument, and panpipe tunes are some of the most joyful in Chinese music.
† Enya (Brennan) is an Irish singer, instrumentalist and composer. She is Ireland's best-selling solo artist and is officially the country's second biggest musical export (after U2). Her works have earned her four Grammy Awards and an Academy Award nomination, and she is also famous for performing in ten different languages during her lengthy career. Enya is an approximate transcription of how Eithne is pronounced in her native Irish, in the Donegal dialect.

letters, one of which came from a young woman who called herself 'Waiter'.

This all happened so many years ago, but it remains fresh in my memory, and comes back to me again, every time I hear Enya's 'Evening Falls'.

'*Dear Xinran . . .*' She was the first of my listeners to address me like this, in fact the first in all my forty years in China. Although I had studied English too, I was still surprised by her bold use of this Westernised form of address. You have to understand that apart from a tiny number of foreign-language students in big cities like Beijing and Shanghai, no one would dare to call – or even think of calling – someone outside their family, or even within it, 'Dear' because the term had been condemned as 'bourgeois sentimentalism' at the start of the Cultural Revolution! Anyway, when I began hosting *Words on the Night Breeze*, none of people who wrote to me every day addressed me as '*Dear*'. Mostly it was '*Comrade Xinran*' or some other respectful Soviet-style form of address.

There followed a long outpouring of twenty pages or more, in which she told her story, which went like this:

Dear Xinran

First of all, thank you for your programme *Words on the Night Breeze*. Every day I wait for it, and every evening it fills my head with thoughts.

How many times, in how many different ways, have you exhorted your listeners not to suffer agonies because of something that happened in the past! You say that we should find in every day the seeds of opportunity for the future, that we should find a quiet space in our minds to fill with plans for our future, because our lives should not be stuck in a past which is dead and gone, and we should use our capacity for living in order to make a better future.

I know you mean well – you don't want good people to throw away their lives today because of pain or remorse they suffered, or mistakes they made, in the past. But even though you used the expression 'suffering agonies', I don't know if you really know what it means to suffer agony. Do you really think people can pick and choose from their past, just the way they move house?

Let me tell you a true story, of someone who has really suffered agonies.

This is the story of a generation of young Chinese women university students, and of a youth lost before it was really enjoyed. Its bitter taste will stay with you for a long time.

'Waiter' is twenty-five, and she has been going out with her boyfriend for two years. He has proposed marriage, but she doesn't dare accept him. She's too scared to face the pre-marriage gynaeco-logical examination,* or even to be honest with her boyfriend about her past. She hardly dares to hope that one day she may be a mother, let alone a grandmother, and is even frightened that the man she loves will hear her crying in her sleep. Because this woman has not just lost her virginity, she's had a baby.

Five years ago, Waiter was accepted for a course in Western culture and languages in the Department of Foreign Languages of a telecommunications college. The college was in the provin-cial capital far from her home town, so Waiter left home to study. Her parents had brought her up strictly, but now she could come and go as she wanted. She read the romantic stories in her text-books, and talked and joked with male students as well as with the girls. In a few short months, these freedoms had gone to her head like wine. Her parents wrote often, the college rules were posted up everywhere and 'worker and peasant cadres' monitored the students' behaviour, but she quickly grew fed up with them. She rejected socially accepted norms of behaviour, especially after she made the shocking discovery that, in order to become Red Guards during the Cultural Revolution, each of her parents had dropped the people that they truly loved; instead, they had obeyed their leaders and married each other, and subsequently aborted a baby, all for the sake of the revolution. She simply could not believe that the parents she had idolised had been so cynical and cowardly. She vowed that she would be like Zhu Yingtai in the old tale 'Butterfly Lovers' and find love for herself. Then she

---

* In one form or another, a check that the hymen was intact had been a pre-marital test for every woman since ancient times. This age-old custom remained mandatory throughout society even in post-Liberation New China, and only finally died out with the reforms of the 1990s.

would, like Jane Eyre, sacrifice everything to defend her love, and would become a girl who lived for love.

Then an enthusiastic young man in his final year began to help her with her English pronunciation and talked to her about great literary masterpieces of the world. Being with him made her pulse race with excitement. Just hearing him breathe felt intoxicating. She was overcome by uncontrollable longings she had never felt before. It was not long before she felt his hand on her shoulder and turned her face up to his. They kissed passionately, over and over, in the corner of the library.

She was awake most of that night in her dormitory bed. As day broke, she fell into an exhausted sleep, and dreamed that a deep voice boomed from the sky: 'You are a bad woman, stealing forbidden fruit.' She woke up but smiled to herself. What was wrong with being a 'bad woman' if she was as lucky as this?

Any Chinese born in the mid-twentieth century knows that most of us were the product of a society where sexual ignorance was rife. We lumped affection, sex and love together as if they were the same thing, we lost our animal instincts and became 'domesticated', there were no accepted standards of right and wrong, and we had no way of knowing what love was or what it meant. In our homes, schools and in society at large, sex education was a dirty word, and was even seen as a family disgrace.

On a cold winter's evening that year, the young lovers took refuge in a kitchen next to the library and, beside the warm crock of bread dough, the girl became a woman and gave her virginity to the first man who had touched her. She wasn't shocked by the blood from her broken hymen – she knew from the dictionary that sacrifice meant giving one's life and one's blood. She was proud and excited to bleed for her lover.

For the next two winter months, they 'proved' the strength of their love next to the warm crock of rising dough over and over again. Their classmates all said they were the hardest-working students in the school because they got back to their dorms so late every night. They were never down on the out-of-school students list, though their names appeared often on the library book borrowing cards. Heaven must have been smiling on them, allowing them to get away with stealing these forbidden fruits, at a time when boys and girls were not allowed to spend time in each other's company.

They were forbidden, nonetheless, and when, two months later, she went home for the Chinese New Year holiday, her period hadn't come. She didn't know what this meant – her parents had not allowed her to have any sex education as she grew up. They lived their lives around her as if they were two work machines. For as long as she could remember, the only way they loved her, the only thing they wanted from her, was that she should study. They didn't even think it was natural that, as a teenager, she should want to look pretty! They constantly warned her that she should 'be strong, have self-respect and live a hard-working, simple life'.

The two weeks of the Chinese New Year holidays seemed like as many years. The first day back at school, she and her boyfriend met beside the dough crock.

After they had made love, her boyfriend held her in his arms and whispered, 'Next time your period comes, let's meet here anyway and hold each other tight. Biology shouldn't get in the way of our love. I'm about to graduate, who knows where I'll be sent to work? I don't want to miss a single evening of our time together.'

She felt overwhelmed with happiness at his words. 'Darling, don't worry,' she murmured. 'I've got a lucky illness, I haven't had a period for two months . . .'

'What? Two months? Aren't you worried?' he pushed himself away from her, held her face and asked urgently.

Her boyfriend seemed so concerned that she felt very emotional, and pressed her lips to his. 'It's nothing,' she said gently. 'It's just that I've been missing you so much, I can't eat or sleep. It's just the kind of lovesickness the Butterfly Lovers had.'

'Well, that's okay then,' he said, holding her tightly. Their love-making that evening left her happier and more satisfied than she had ever been before. However, something very strange happened after that. Her boyfriend didn't come to the library for days. After about two weeks, she could bear it no longer. She had never been to his classroom before, or even to his year group. They had agreed that they had to keep their relationship a secret.

If they were discovered, they would not only be punished, they would also be forced to separate. But she was heedless of that now. She searched for him everywhere, but everyone told her that he'd left and transferred to another school. They said it was so that he would be allocated a better job. He'd pulled strings and got himself into a university in Beijing even before graduating.

Gone away? Without a word to her? Her beloved boyfriend who had told her how much he loved her, who had made love to her! She was shocked and confused. It must be a bad dream. But her ever-swelling abdomen finally woke her up to reality: she was pregnant!

The horrified realisation that she was pregnant and unmarried brought her down to earth. She was panic-stricken, beside herself with anxiety. The person she most loved had disappeared from her life, but another life was being born in her body. She went out and bought heaps of surgical bandages and, concealed behind her mosquito net, bound her abdomen tightly every night. A philosopher once said that creatures which have to fight for life have the most tenacious genes. The foetus in her belly may have been a social outcast, but it was demanding its right to life. No bandage was going to stop it from growing.

The weather grew hotter and hotter, and the baggy, concealing jumpers she wore made her pour with sweat. But her fellow students were as ignorant as she was, if not more so. She said she was a southerner and felt the cold even in summer, and no one asked any more questions. They were too busy studying anyway. One day, she couldn't bear the heat any more and asked for permission to go and lie down in the dormitory. Three fellow students were there but when they had gone, she took off her clothes to cool down. Suddenly, the cleaning woman came in – to be confronted by the sight of the student's unmistakably pregnant belly. The two of them stared dumbly at each other.

The cleaner sighed and asked gently, 'How many months is it?'

'What do you mean?' She frowned, trying to work out what the question meant.

'How many months since you last had a period?'

'Five months!' she replied, pulling on a winter cotton over-jacket.

'Child, you're pregnant!' The cleaner sounded serious.

'I know!' Waiter said coolly, buttoning her jacket up.

'But . . . why?' the cleaner asked in a mixture of concern and agitation.

That 'why?' sounded accusing to Waiter. She'd never met the woman before, and she resented a stranger putting pressure on her. Then she said stiffly, 'I've no one to turn to. My parents will kill me, the school will kick me out, and everyone will call me a slut!'

'What about him? Hasn't he done anything to get you out of this mess?'

'Him? He's disappeared!' she said in a sudden burst of anger.

'Disappeared! He . . .' The cleaner could not help sounding shrill.

But Waiter interrupted her. 'I don't want to talk about him. You wouldn't understand.'

'Child, I don't know how you educated people carry on your love affairs, but I know what this is all about. I can help you.'

'Help me how?'

'My parents live in a small town not far away, and my aunt is a doctor in the local immunisation clinic. She can give you an abortion.'

'You want me to have an abortion?! Kill a tiny living creature? No, no, I can't!' But Waiter's convictions came only from what she had read in books and her own naïvety. Not only did she have no one to share her secret with, she didn't even know enough to be able to make a proper decision or protect herself.

The cleaner looked at a small alarm clock attached to her apron and said anxiously, 'Then how are you going to have a baby here? What will the school say, let alone your parents? You're being stupid, you've got to think this through! I'm going to finish cleaning the other rooms, and then I'll come back.'

Conflicting thoughts raced through Waiter's head, but eventually she accepted the cleaner's suggestion. She forged a letter saying her father was seriously ill, and asked for leave. Then she went to stay with the cleaner's parents.

This couple had had their land requisitioned by the government, and made a living from cleaning and polishing the fittings in a hotel. Only an unmarried daughter remained at home, while the rest of their children had gone off to find work in the big city. They were simple folk, honest and kind. When their relative, the doctor, did the pre-op blood test, she found that Waiter's platelet count was low. Concerned that she might haemorrhage, the doctor prescribed some medicine and persuaded the young woman to wait a couple of weeks before having the abortion. To build up her strength, the couple killed all their laying hens, one after another, bought supplements and tonics, and made nourishing soups for her every day. A few weeks later, she finally lay on the operating table. As the doctor completed her pre-op checks, she said regretfully, 'It's a fine, healthy foetus, quite a big one. See how vigorously it's moving.'

Waiter dissolved into tears, overcome with guilt. She could almost hear the baby's indignant cries: 'Why? Why do you want to kill me?' She didn't know where she got the strength from, but she found herself on her feet, shouting, 'No, I can't do it. I can't kill my child!'

Filled with determination, she got out all the money her parents had given her and pushed it into the couple's hands. 'Please let me have my baby here!'

She gave birth to a full-term baby – a plump, fair-skinned daughter. She called her 'Mei' 逃 , meaning that this quiet little thing had survived misfortune. The couple only shook their heads in puzzlement. They had never come across this obscure Chinese character before.

When the Birth Month* was up, the cleaner put a big envelope into her hands. It contained a Missing Person notice put out by the school, a letter saying that she had been expelled for forging the letter about her father's illness, and some letters from her parents, first worried as to her whereabouts, and then announcing to her and the school that they were cutting her off.

She had not only been expelled from the school for her

---

* Traditionally, in China, the woman is expected to have complete rest for a month after birth; she is confined to the house, and given an especially nutritious diet. Mother and baby are expected to remain indoors, to avoid cold winds and viruses, and the mother may not bath or shower in case she catches a chill. (*Trans.*)

wickedness, she had also so disgraced her parents, to whom 'face' was everything, that they wanted nothing more to do with her. The only family she had left was herself and a four-week-old daughter.

Cradling her daughter in her arms, Waiter tearfully read the letters one by one. When she had finished, the cleaner said, 'Give the baby to my parents to look after. You're on your own, with no husband or family. How are you going to manage otherwise?'

'No, I couldn't be so selfish. Your parents have been so helpful to me, I can't ask them to do any more. If it had been a boy, they could have taken him in to give the family some extra support, but no one values girls around here. Besides, your parents are getting on in years, and they're still working all hours to make a living and put a bit by for when they're old. I couldn't impose an extra burden on them.'

And Waiter took Mei, then just six weeks old and, following the tide of humanity set in motion by Deng Xiaoping's economic reforms, went down south to Guangdong. There, far from her family and memories of the past, she hoped to make a fresh start.

The reality, however, was just as the cleaner had predicted: it was impossible for a woman with no husband or family and encumbered with a baby to get work. In factory dormitories, girls slept seven or eight to a room. They had little enough time to rest from the hard work and overtime they did. Having a fussing, crying baby in the dormitory as well was too much for them. As for renting a place on her own, no child-minder would be willing to squeeze into a single room with her mistress; by now her savings were almost gone and she could not, even in her wildest dreams, afford to rent an extra room for the child-minder.

For a while, she struggled to make ends meet, but finally had to face the fact that her little baby was losing weight and becoming weaker. As a last resort, she left Mei at the door of an orphanage in Guangzhou, capital of Guangdong province, in the hope that the welfare services would look after her. She hid some distance away and, rooted to the spot, watched as the staff picked the baby up. She hoped to hear her daughter's cries one more time, but Mei made no sound at all. Was it possible that this tiny girl understood enough to try and spare her mother more grief?

The second her daughter had disappeared through the gate of the orphanage, Waiter made a dash for the station knowing that if she did not, she would find herself knocking and asking for her daughter back. In a corner of the station waiting room, she cried inconsolably. Bystanders gathered round, then gradually dispersed, leaving her to herself. Clutching her daughter's little milk-stained bib, she left for Zhuhai.

Four months later, she finally obtained her first long-term work contract. Taking an overnight train back to Guangzhou, she rushed back to the orphanage – to find that it and her daughter had disappeared, leaving behind nothing but a heap of rubble. The building, she was told, had been demolished, and the orphanage closed down.

Closed down? What about the orphans? Nobody knew. She ran madly from one government office to another, from the local Neighbourhood Committee to the City Government offices, from the Planning Department to the Demolition Department, but no one could tell her where the orphanage children had gone.

In China in those days, there were so many things that remained unexplained.

Xinran, can you understand the feelings of that woman who had lost her daughter? Never to be happy again, condemned to live in silent agony – can you imagine that? Can you make the memories of her daughter fade as she goes through life?

Waiter, the woman who waits, is me. That's the name I gave myself after I lost my daughter – not 'waiter' in the sense of someone who waits at tables in a restaurant, but meaning someone who waits for a future which will never come. Before, I didn't know I was waiting, I just knew I was doing penance and being punished by God. Don't get me wrong, I'm not a religious person, but I dare not believe that God doesn't exist, because I'm being punished! Not a day goes by without me thinking of her. I can't help myself, I always look at any girl walking by, even if she's too old or young. After all, that girl – so close I could reach out and touch her – might be Mei! I can't bear to watch TV advertisements for children's products. The mother and child in the picture should be me and my family, but I'll never get my family back. I can't read a book or listen to music on my own

– my daughter comes alive with the melody and on the pages as I read. I miss Mei so much, my life has turned into a desolate, uninhabited island. Every night I call to her from my island: 'How are you, baby? Do you know that your mother, the woman who gave you life and has given you her life too, is thinking about you? You sucked from her breast not just milk, but your mother's very soul. Where are you? Your disappearance has imprisoned me in memories. Come back to me! Across the barriers of time, come and let me touch your face, let me see you alive and free!'

I'm two different people now. By day, I'm just like any other woman of my age, working away like mad, wanting recognition for everything, from the way I look and dress to my intelligence and my work. I long for love, and I do love my boyfriend. But by night, I become the lonely woman I have grown into, weighed down with the guilt of having abandoned my daughter. The pain of missing her so much tears me apart, until sometimes I actually feel it's giving me a real, physical heart attack.

Xinran, do you really think I can walk away from the past which my daughter has given me, simply efface it from memory, and live in the present and face the future?

And she signed herself, 'Waiter, a mother in agony'.

*

That afternoon, I sat down as usual to prepare *Words on the Night Breeze*. In those days, broadcasters were governed by a number of injunctions: we were not to discuss religion, stories from the Western media, 'free' ideas not strictly in line with the Chinese government's thinking, proposals for an independent judicial system, the private lives of government leaders, and sex. I marked excerpts from Waiter's letter with my red pen and worked out how I was going to read this letter on air without breaking down in tears, and also without breaking the rules. However, as the tape of Enya's music began to turn and my programme started, I suddenly found it impossible to read out even the excerpts I had chosen. How could I calmly reproduce the cries of love she had addressed to her daughter? What kind of a response to her distress was that?

I got a grip on myself, choked back the tears and read the bits out as sympathetically as I could, to a little girl who probably had no idea who her mother was. My hope was that people would hear it and understand, wherever they were, and would provide this desperate mother with the hoped-for news.

However, not a single one of the hundreds of letters I received after the programme told her anything worth hearing.

Perhaps I should not admit this to my readers, but to be perfectly honest, most of the responses to Waiter's predicament were unsympathetic. They mocked her, condemned her, and some of them even expressed surprise that she should be so shameless as to tell everyone about her 'sluttish' behaviour.

I do not believe that those who blamed her were incapable of sympathy. I think that a lifetime of exposure to traditional Chinese cultural values had conditioned their nature as human beings. The 'commandments' which governed many people's lives had effectively excised their normal human instincts, so that they were unable to acknowledge love.

The way we understand both our present and our future depends on what we have lived through.

The first two years after I came to London on my own, I was drawn every weekend into my local McDonald's by the shouts and laughter of the throngs of children. I had had to leave Panpan behind with my parents in Nanjing, first as I struggled to decide whether I could make my future in the West, and then while I tried to establish myself in London. The ache of missing him was with me every day. As I sat and thought longingly of the son whom I had been unable to bring with me, the agonised voice of that mother rang in my ears:

'*How are you, baby? Do you know that your mother, the woman who gave you life and has given you her life too, is thinking about you? You sucked from her breast not just milk, but your mother's very soul. Where are you? Your disappearance has imprisoned me in memories. Come back to me! Across the barriers of time, come and let me touch your face, let me see you alive and free!*'

However, I was much more fortunate than Waiter. Two years after leaving China, I held my son Panpan in my arms again and was released from the hell of my own longing.

I still do not know whether Waiter ever told her boyfriend the truth. If she got married, did her husband discover the person his wife turned into in her nightmares? If so, did they dare acknowledge this daughter openly? This would not only mean flouting social norms; the one-child policy would also ensure that they would never be able to have a child of their own. The 'agonised' mother might even find herself being disciplined by her employers. No one around her would ever respect her again, no matter how outstanding a person she was. How many Chinese women down the ages have been destroyed in this way?

This is why, after that broadcast, whenever I heard Enya's music I always recalled that woman. She is probably still waiting for a daughter who must be in her twenties now, just about the age that her mother was when she gave birth. Old people in China say you never know how much your parents loved you until you become a parent yourself. Has Waiter's daughter begun to understand her birth mother's feelings? She has probably never been told who she really is and where she came from.

I have never forgotten Waiter. She is not just there in Enya's evocative music; she and her story brought into sharp focus a new question which I have been mulling over ever since. With all the dramatic changes China has undergone, will women forced by tradition to abandon their girl babies ever get the chance to hold them in their arms again?

2

'The Mothers of Girls Are All Heartsick'

'But there's something I want to ask you. Can you tell me how to have a baby boy?'

IN 1989, I made my first visit to a very poor region on the north bank of the middle reaches of the Yellow River. As I interviewed the local peasants, a woman of about thirty with three children in tow asked me: 'Have you ever "done" a girl baby?' At first I thought the question had something to do with childcare or housework . . .

'What did you say? "Do" a girl baby? What on earth does that mean?' I thought I must have misheard the local accent again.

'You don't even know how to do a girl baby . . . and you're a woman?!' She was as mystified as I was. 'If you don't know that, then what do you do if your baby's a girl? Get someone else to do it, or what?'

'I, er . . . I haven't got a daughter.' I still did not understand.

'"Doing" a girl baby is getting rid of it at birth!' the local policeman who had come with me told me helpfully.

'What? Killing a girl baby! But why?' Now I was completely confused.

'You can't *not* do girl babies, unless you only give birth to boys. Your husband's family would never forgive you. They'd make your life a misery! They'd beat you, and you'd never get

33

enough to eat!' The woman was clearly astonished that there were women in the world who did not know about 'doing' girl babies.

*

As time went by, and I travelled around China gathering material for programmes, I found out that the old village custom of 'doing' girl babies to death was extremely common in provinces such as Henan, Shandong, Anhui, Jiangxi, Hunan, Shaanxi, Shanxi and Northern Jiangsu. They had different terms for it, depending on where you were, and the ways of disposing of the babies was different, but there was no avoiding the fact that it was a normal part of a woman's life, just as that peasant woman had said. These brutal folk customs left me speechless, yet I still wanted to know whether these mothers for whom it was common practice really smothered their daughters as casually as they ate a meal or threw away a piece of rotten fruit. Of course, they did not. People might say that a woman who abandons her baby must have a heart of stone, but everything I saw and heard told me this was almost never the case. Those women loved their babies just as much as any other mother. As a Shandong woman in her fifties once said to me: 'Any woman who's had a baby has felt pain, and the mothers of girls are all heartsick too!'

I met this woman in 1989 while doing a story in the Yimeng Mountain* area of Shandong province. There were four of us in our group, and we were to eat dinner at the house of the head of the village. As we went into the yard, he indicated a strip of roughly woven blue-and-white material about 5 cm wide and 20 cm long, fluttering in the wind over the entrance. 'It's to tell people the family's going to have a baby, and we don't want to be disturbed!'

---

* Yimeng Mountain villages are isolated and road communications are poor. The villagers have little to sell to the outside world, and consequently no money to buy anything in. During the Anti-Japanese War and the War of Liberation, nearly 200,000 local people joined the People's Liberation Army, and nearly every family sacrificed one of its members. Yet extreme poverty persists: the lack of natural resources and effective government policies meant that as late as the 1990s, nearly half the villagers had an average net yearly income of less than 200 yuan (about £20 at 2009 rates), making this one of the areas in China with the highest concentration of poor households.

This peasant family's small courtyard followed the local pattern. There were low mud-brick buildings on three sides; the parents' rooms were in the middle facing the gate, the married son had an inner and an outer room on the right side, while the unmarried children's rooms were on the left side, together with storage for the farm implements and animal fodder. The parents were the only ones with a kitchen, a large room adjoining the bedroom where all the family members ate. Cooking and other household utensils were piled on the floor; there was also a table about a metre square and a dozen or so stools of varying sizes – too many to be accommodated at the table. Actually, in most poor mountain areas in north China, people do not bother to use the table. They just squat, holding a bowl of thin soup, a dry flat bread and piece of pickled vegetable all in one hand; there are usually no other dishes to put on the table.

We had scarcely sat down in the kitchen when we heard a moan of pain from the bedroom next door. The village head's wife, the one who told me 'Any woman who's had a baby has felt pain, and the mothers of girls are all heartsick too!' said politely: 'Pay no attention. My daughter-in-law is in labour. We'll just eat our dinner.'

'Do you need any help?' I offered, equally politely.

'No, no, I couldn't let you city cadres get your hands dirty. Please eat. I'm afraid it's only poor country food, fried egg yam pancake. The flour-paste soup will be ready in a bit and I'll bring it in. Eat up, please! The midwife's with her and I've heated up water, but I don't know if she'll be using it yet!'

I had only made a few trips to villages at that time, and I was painfully aware how little I knew about local customs, let alone the local dialects, which sounded different every couple of miles. I have to admit that I only half understood what the woman was saying. What were yam pancakes and flour-paste soup? What was she heating the water for? And why did she not know whether it was going to be used or not?

One of the policemen who had accompanied us, seeing I was about to ask more stupid questions, pushed me into a seat in the corner and whispered into my ear, 'They do things differently here. Don't ask any more questions or it will get me into trouble

with my bosses.' Once I heard the words 'They do things differently here', I did not dare say any more. In China, it is not just
that the dialect changes every couple of miles; every twenty-five
miles or so, you find different customs. You may offend against
local taboos without meaning to, however well-intentioned you
are.

The cries from the inner room grew louder – the woman was
bearing the pain bravely. I heard another woman's voice saying,
in something like *putonghua*, 'It's crowning. Pant! Push hard!'*
The very words made me break out in a sweat. I am a mother,
and I felt for her. She was probably feeling she'd be better off
dead. Suddenly, the noise rose in a crescendo – and abruptly
stopped. There was a low sob, and then a man's gruff voice said
accusingly: 'Useless thing!'

The two policemen on either side of me obviously guessed what
was going through my 'liberated' city-girl's mind and, as one, they
pinned me into the corner where I sat. Behind me there was a
covered slops pail, and some foul-smelling containers of animal
feed. I was puzzled about what was going on in the other room.
Normally, we should have heard the baby cry, shouldn't we? But
there was no sound. The village head and his wife sat looking
embarrassed, not to say downright disheartened.

Soon, a young man of about twenty came out, his head bowed,
took a bowl of the flour-paste soup and went back inside again.
As we watched him, I heard a stifled whimper in the corner
behind me and, turning round, saw the woman who was obviously the midwife wiping her hands on her apron. The village
head gave her a small envelope containing her fee and she hurried
away.

Suddenly, I thought I heard a slight movement in the slops pail
behind me, and automatically glanced towards it. I felt ice in my
blood. To my absolute horror, I saw a tiny foot poking out of
the pail. I couldn't believe what I was seeing. Then the tiny foot
twitched! It wasn't possible. The midwife must have dropped that
tiny baby alive into the slop pail! I nearly threw myself at it, but

* i.e. standard Chinese, not dialect. Midwives travelled around from village to village
and so had to communicate in *putonghua*. (*Trans.*)

the two policemen held my shoulders in a firm grip. 'Don't move, you can't save it, it's too late!'

'But that's . . . murder . . . and you're the police!' I was aghast.

We sat in silence while I stared, sickened, at the pail. It seemed to me that everything stopped around me. The little foot was still now. The policemen held on to me for a few more minutes.

'Let's go and have a pipe in the courtyard. It reeks of blood here!' said the village head man finally, dragging the policemen outside. They released their hold on me and went out. The only people left now were the head's wife and I, and, in the inner room, the woman who had just given birth with the young man who had taken her some soup. But I couldn't move.

'Doing a baby girl is not a big thing around here. You city folk are shocked the first time you see it, right?' the older woman said comfortingly, obviously seeing how shocked I was.

'That's a living child!' I said in a shaking voice, pointing at the slops pail. I was still so shocked, I didn't dare to move.

'It's not a child,' she corrected me.

'What do you mean, it's not a child? I saw it.' I could scarcely believe that she could tell me such a blatant lie!

'It's not a child. If it was, we'd be looking after it, wouldn't we?' she interrupted. 'It's a girl baby, and we can't keep it.'

'A girl baby isn't a child, and you can't keep it?' I repeated uncomprehendingly.

'Around these parts, you can't get by without a son. You have no one to burn incense at the ancestors' shrine. But it's not just that. You don't get the extra land given to you either. If your children just eat, and don't earn, and you have no land and no grain, then you might as well starve!' She looked at me and added: 'You city folk get food from the government. We get our grain ration according to the number of people in the family. Girl babies don't count. The officials in charge don't give us any extra land when a girl is born, and there's so little arable land that the girls will starve to death anyway.'

This was 1989, and I did not know until then that a system for allocating land which went back 2,000 years was still in use in Chinese villages near the end of the twentieth century. I certainly had no idea that, because of it, so many baby girls had lost the right to life.

'Any woman who's had a baby has felt pain, and the mothers of girls are all heartsick too!' the head's wife said as she carried another bowl of flour-paste soup into the bedroom.

I could only sit there, dumbly watching over that slops pail and the tiny life in it, scarcely born and so quickly snuffed out. In such a hurry to depart, and so alone. Just because she was a girl! 'The mothers of girls are all heartsick!' The words have echoed in my ears down the years. And the memory of that small, twitching foot still often disturbs my dreams ... Could I have saved her?

*

About two years later, a young peasant couple came to the radio station to see me. They were looking for work in the city, and told me that they were the parents of the baby thrown into the slops pail, whom I had met in the Yimeng Mountains. I had never seen the woman but I recognised the man as the one who had come out of the inner room to take his wife a bowl of soup. Two years of hard farm work seemed to have aged him at least ten years. I gave them lunch in a noodle restaurant and then the man went off to sign up for a job. I sat there with his wife and we talked for a couple of hours.

She sat there rather stiffly so, to put her at her ease, I started by asking about her family. 'How are your parents-in-law?'

'Very well, thank you.'

'Are they still hard at work on the land?'

'Busier than ever.'

'Why?'

'Because all the men of the village have gone off to the cities to get labouring jobs. Like my husband.'

'So just the women are left?'

'Only the old people and the children still work on the land. This year, the women have left too, for the first time.'

'Do the old people and the children cope?'

'They have to. If their families live near enough to a road, the workers go back to help get the harvest in. If the village is off the beaten track, then they're in trouble. If they don't plant their fields, the village government takes the land away from them. If they don't harvest what they've got, then they don't get the government grain ration, and the land is taken away too, so how are they going to live?'

'Now that you two have left, are your parents doing all the farm work?'

'They have to. The government started saying this year that if you have no land, you can get a job in the city. We have to go wherever the work is. That's what my father-in-law said. And if the family doesn't have a son, it has no roots. You can't hold your head up, you're good for nothing. If the family has no roots, then it's finished! So my father-in-law told us to leave, and come back with a son!

'We didn't want to have to listen to the other villagers gossiping, so we stayed away from the construction sites where they work. My father-in-law said people are educated in a big city, so he told us to come here. We haven't come to ask you for help, my husband's already got work. But there's something I want to ask you. Can you tell me how to have a baby boy?'

'Me?' I told her truthfully that I did not have that kind of knowledge, but I had heard lots of city folk say that you can tell what the baby will be by what the mother likes eating in pregnancy: acidic foods mean a boy, and hot, spicy food means a girl. I had also heard there were herbs you could take to help conceive a boy. I had never tried them myself so I did not know whether they worked. I advised her to get work cleaning vegetables or killing chickens in the market. She might find someone there who had some tips for her. But I warned her that nothing was sure.

'Do you still think about your daughter?' I asked her. She knew I meant the baby in the slops pail.

'Of course I do! That was my first child, and I didn't even set eyes on her. I just heard two little grunts, and then she was thrown away.' She sounded annoyed but not particularly sad.

'So you've had a boy now?' I guessed.

'No, we haven't. Otherwise we wouldn't have left home. But

39

there was such gossip in the village, it was unbearable.' She hung her head, and seemed ashamed, as if she had done something wrong.

'You mean you've had no more children?' I was worried she might have suffered some injury that had stopped her conceiving.

'I had two more, but they were both girls, and my father-in-law gave them to foreigners,' she said helplessly. Even now her face showed no sadness, but I asked myself what she felt in her heart about the loss.

'Gave them to foreigners? What does that mean?' Up till then I had not heard of foreigners adopting Chinese children, as there had been no coverage in the Chinese media.

'My parents-in-law said it was better to have them adopted by foreigners than to kill them. They'd go far away overseas and no one would know about them! After we did the first girl, I left the village and hid somewhere else to have the second two. We just told everyone we were going to the city to find work. We thought we would have a son and go home, but the next two were girls. My father-in-law got someone to take the babies south, and told us they'd be adopted by foreigners.' Still she didn't look up.

'Do you know what kind of foreigners?' These peasants knew all about it but we reporters had never heard of such a thing, so I was keen to know more. Overseas adoption of Chinese children officially began in 1993, and yet it seemed migrant workers in south China were talking about it as early as 1990. There has always been talk that overseas adoptions started before 1993, but the government has always denied it.

'I don't know. My father-in-law said they were foreigners with coloured eyes* and big noses. It sounds so scary, my daughters must be terrified! Have you seen any foreigners?' She looked up at me expectantly.

'Yes, I have, in books, in pictures and on the street. Most foreigners are good people, and they like children,' I said as encouragingly as I could.

'My daughters were both as good as gold. The eldest was with me for the whole of the Birth Month. She was such a good feeder,

---
* i.e. blue, green or hazel eyes. (*Trans.*)

40

she loved her milk! I don't know if she'd have liked the foreigner's milk as much. The second one was taken away in less than three weeks so as to catch a foreigner who was waiting for a baby. It was all done in such a hurry, I didn't have time to tell the people who came for her to pass the message on that she slept best if you held her in your left arm. Do you think the foreigners know how to hold my baby? I can't do anything about the baby who was "done" and died, but the next two lived, and I'm so worried about them. My heart hurts whenever I think about them. My husband says I'm heartsick.' At this, she seized the front of the jacket she wearing, as if she was trying to ease the pain in the heart tucked inside it.

'Foreigners are just like you and me, they know what children need. All women anywhere have maternal instincts, we're all like the Guan Yin inside.'* The poor woman was racked with anxiety, and these were the only words I could think of to comfort her.

'What's maternal instincts?' she asked. Then she rushed on: 'I can't read or write. But I came here to see if I could bump into the foreigners who adopted my daughters. Besides, I heard that city folk know how to have a baby boy. I thought I could learn that too, have a boy and then go home and live like a human being for a bit!' This woman really had grown up in the belief that 'you do not count as a human being unless you have a son'.

I told her that maternal instincts meant what her mother-in-law had said: 'Any woman who's had a baby has felt pain, and the mothers of girls are all heartsick too!'

'Is your mother-in-law married to the eldest son in the family?'† I asked her, eager to find out more about someone from the older generation who could see so deeply into other women's hearts.

'Yes, otherwise how would she know what I was feeling? She told me how she was heartsick too. I think she was worried that I might get depressed. She's not a bad woman, and she's suffered a lot. She told me she had six terrible years when she gave birth to four girls and "did" them all, before she had a son. She told me that everything was a mess back then, there was nothing to

---

* The Buddhist Goddess of Mercy. (*Trans.*)
† This would make it even more important for her to produce a male heir. (*Trans.*)

41

eat and no money so you couldn't leave. The cadres were even tougher, and if you didn't work in the fields you were counter-revolutionary. She couldn't bring herself to "do" her first daughter, but she did the second, third and fourth herself. The villagers said she was so good at "doing" girl babies, it was over in no time at all. My husband was her only son. After that she had several more girls and they kept all of them. My father-in-law was a cadre so, on the quiet, he managed to get a few scraps more land for himself and his family, but my mother-in-law says she was always hungry. She never let her children go hungry, though. Two of my sisters-in-law were the only girls in the village to go to school. The other parents couldn't afford it. My mother-in-law said that if you had a bit of schooling and married a city man who could read and write too, then it wouldn't matter if you didn't have a son.'

'Do you believe her?' I asked. I wondered if I would believe that if I had grown up in a village like hers.

'Of course I do! She's a good woman and she's very kind at heart. She never beat me or left me without food. A good mother-in-law is hard to come by. For a woman like me who can't have a son, I don't have any way out, do I? If you don't believe me, go and ask any other woman.'

I had to leave her then to get back to work. I can still picture that woman waiting there, for her husband to return – and still waiting for a son.

*

During my many years of research into the lives of Chinese women, I found it extremely hard to get my hands on the kind of documentary evidence that would have been held by central or local governments in the developed world. This was partly because anything 'old' was looted and destroyed during the Cultural Revolution. More importantly, however, Chinese women down the ages have never had the right to tell their own stories. They lived on the bottom rung of society, unquestioning obedience was expected of them and they had no means of building lives of their own. So 'natural' had this become that most women wished for only two things – not to give birth to daughters in this life, and not to be reborn as a woman in the next.

Many women, especially in poor country areas, suffered so much it made them indifferent or even cruel to other women. They did not believe that their own daughters could escape this vicious circle either, yet they did not want to see them 'bring disgrace' on the family, or suffer the same sad fate as had been inflicted on themselves. So sometimes, in an act of love, they 'put them out of their misery' by smothering them at birth. Times may have changed in China but many mothers, especially those in poor urban and country areas, have continued to face the same choices; this, it seemed, was part of being a woman and a mother.

3

The Midwife's Story

'If I could see it was going to be a boy, and it was the first-born, then it was an "incense birth". I could quote three times the normal rate for that.'

IT WAS Waiter's letter which opened my eyes to the fact that women got rid of their babies, and my experience in the Yimeng Mountain village which first brought me into direct contact with one of those mothers. The first time I came across an abandoned baby was, however, on a winter's morning in 1990.

I had a lot on at work. At eleven in the morning I had a strategy meeting and at three in the afternoon, the usual political study session. I also had to fit in a special guest interview before my *Words on the Night Breeze* in the evening, so I decided to go to the radio station early to prepare the topics and the music, and to read and edit listeners' letters.

It was barely light and bitterly cold as I rode my Flying Pigeon bicycle to work at eight o'clock that morning. My hands were frozen even though I was wearing gloves, and many of the people hurrying to work wore face masks. (When, in 1997, I arrived in the West and read in the newspapers that the Chinese wore face masks to protect them against city air pollution, I could not help laughing. Before 1990, the vast majority of Chinese did not know what environmental pollution was. In the early years of economic reform, the busiest construction sites were all in southern coastal cities. In the hinterland, we were still playing 'wait and see'.

Large-scale urban reconstruction did not begin for us until the late 1990s. Winter temperatures in our continental climate plunged to minus 10 or even down to minus 30, so people wore masks to protect their faces against the cold. I did not much like wearing a mask, for three reasons: my ears were too delicate and the mask would not stay on; it made my glasses mist up; and the inner layer very soon got unpleasantly damp.)

My bicycle rides, as I wove my way through the street markets and the alleyways far from the main thoroughfares, taught me invaluable lessons about the society I was living in. Until the end of the 1970s you saw the sort of queues which you never see nowadays: every morning as soon as it was light, long lines of people formed in the still-empty food market, waiting for the meat, oil and bean curd shops to open, because in those days there were more ration coupons than there were basic necessities (fuel, rice, oil and salt) to go around. No one read a book or the newspaper – the only news then was Party news, and it would be broadcast to everyone anyway. There was no pushing and shoving to get the best bargains – that would have got you shot for 'imperialist behaviour'. So did people chat to while away the long hours spent queuing? Certainly not! Lots of people had been imprisoned for 'idle chatter'! The only time voices were raised was when we shouted political slogans. We never talked about everyday life.

By the 1980s, there was plenty of basic fuel and foodstuffs to be bought, but not much choice as regards quality or price. A decade later, the main streets of most towns and cities had been transformed by the economic boom but its effects had not percolated into the side streets where ordinary people did their shopping. There was something else which had not changed: the lines of people snaking down the street in the early morning. In rumpled clothes, sleepy-eyed and hunched up against the cold, they stood in long, impatient queues outside stinking public toilets, some of which leaked raw sewage, loudly berating the people inside for taking too long. There was no avoiding those toilets, though I would have liked to. There was one on almost every street – just the one, for over a hundred residents.

On that day, just as I was passing one such toilet, instead of the usual queue I saw a crowd of people jostling each other around the entrance. I realised something must have happened. There was little enough entertainment in China in those days, as the media was tightly controlled and most people did not have their own TV or phone, or money to go to the theatre or cinema (actually there was almost nothing to go and see anywhere, even if you had the money). So for most people the only entertainment, and their only chance to participate in 'the news', was when something out of the ordinary happened in the street and they could stand around gawping. This particular crowd must have been made up of the entire population of the street. I kept my finger on the bicycle bell and began to wheel the bicycle through. Everyone was talking at once, and what with the pushing and shoving in front and behind me, I could only inch my way forward.

I finally reached the place where the crowd was thickest. An argument seemed to be going on, and bits of it drifted towards me:

'Ai-ya! What a tiny thing. It must be premature.'

'Ai-yaw! Look, it seems to be breathing! Maybe it's still alive!'

'Of course it is! Look at its little head squirming, poor little thing!'

'It must be a girl. Its mother must have wanted it to live, otherwise she would have dumped it down the toilet.'

'I don't think the little mite can last much longer, it's such a cold day, it'll snuff it soon. Look, it's going blue, it can't hold out much longer . . .'

I had never heard a discussion like this before, and felt some trepidation. I wondered what on earth was going on.

My bicycle and I finally broke through the circle. There was something lying at our feet, something tightly swaddled from head to toe in cheap, blue-and-white patterned cloth. Its tiny head – no bigger than my fist – was a bluish colour, but still twitching now and then, and it struggled for breath. It was a baby, and it was still alive!

'Hey, look, it's still moving!' The shout went up from the bystanders, but no one picked the baby up. I do not know how long it had been lying there, but judging by the size of the crowd and how cold *they* looked, it must have been quite a long time.

Why? Were these people so lacking in humanity that they could watch an infant freeze to death in front of them without lifting a finger to help? I just shoved my bicycle at someone in the crowd, made a dive for the baby, picked her up and tucked her inside the front of my leather coat. There was uproar.

'What is she doing?'

'Is she going to take the baby away with her?'

'Does she know what she's doing? What an idiot. You can't go doing things like that!'

'Young people are so impetuous. Easy enough to pick it up, but how will she get rid of it?!'

I did not pay much attention. Holding the bundle tucked into the front of my coat, I fished inside my shoulder bag for a name card, and gave it to the astonished young man who was holding my bicycle. 'Please ride it to the radio station for me. I'm presenting the evening programme. Before it starts, I'll wait for you at Reception and give you something for bringing it to me. Thank you!' I did not wait for his answer, but ran with the infant to the nearby hospital. In those days, few taxis would try and get down those narrow side streets.

'The little mite can't last much longer . . .' The words rang in my ears, but I kept repeating to myself: 'No, no, I'm not going to let this tiny creature die in front of my eyes. This is a human being. A real live human being capable of giving life to countless other lives.'

I rushed into the hospital Emergency Department, and straight to the Registration window. The Registration nurse stopped me: 'Excuse me, is this your baby? Do you have its birth permit? Without the birth permit, we can't treat it.'

'I'm sorry, I don't know about that. I've just picked her up outside a public toilet. Look, she's blue with cold. I want a doctor to check her over, and save the little thing.' I held the baby up against the glass, in the hope that seeing it might stir her maternal instincts.

'I'm sorry but without the birth permit, we can't register it. And if it's not registered, no doctor will treat it. They get bonuses based on the number of patients registered!'* The tiny swaddled bundle I held in front of her had obviously had no effect.

---

* Bonuses were several times the basic wage in the 1980s.

'Saving lives is a doctor's duty! I can't believe you're going to stand here and watch this baby die in front of your eyes!' I said, more fiercely now. Time was of the essence, she should know that.

'You're quite right, but doctors are human too. If they go against the rules and regulations and lose their jobs, are you going to take responsibility?'

I could see that arguing was getting me nowhere. I opened my shoulder bag, took out my Press Card and pushed it against the window: 'Take a good look at this. I'm going to do a news report on this baby. What's more important in China today – a human life, or the system you're talking about? If this baby dies today in your hospital, I'm going to report it on the programme tonight and it'll be in the papers tomorrow. I wonder what your bosses will have to say about that!' Journalists at that time had surprising power, and she knew it.

She looked terrified by my tirade, and clearly did not know what to do.

'Please fetch your supervisor. Otherwise, I'll make an immediate report to the provincial radio station and in half an hour the news will be all over the town.'

'I'll go and tell the supervisor,' the nurse said, and she hung a 'Registration Closed' notice on the window. Then she hurried off to ask what to do.

A few minutes later a middle-aged doctor arrived, and without a word, took the baby from me. He carried it into the Emergency Treatment Room, but stopped me following him and motioned for me to wait outside. I had just sat down when a man wearing a hospital coat came up to me.

'Excuse me, are you Xinran from the radio station?'

'Yes, what is it?' I demanded, my hackles up. I was still infuriated by my rejection at the Registration window.

'I'm the duty nurse in charge here, and the manager has asked me to come and explain what happened at Registration. The nurse followed correct procedures but she should have been more flexible in her approach. Our hospital has a responsibility to carry out our work in accordance with the government's one-child policy, and Maternity and Paediatrics are critical departments.

No hospital personnel have the right to flout that policy. If we did, we'd all lose our jobs,' he explained gently.

'What if it means injury to a human life? Doesn't saving life override hospital regulations?' I retorted stubbornly.

'Of course it does. That's common sense, and we doctors and nurses are human beings with feelings too. In the past we saved the lives of many babies abandoned outside the hospital, almost all of them girls. But we couldn't keep them here. We had to send them to the orphanage. Then the orphanage said they couldn't take any more, there were too many abandoned babies. No one was giving them more money or staff to look after them, as the orphanage was already well over quota! We have no formal adoption system here. We hospital staff would like to take these babies in ourselves but if we already have a child, the one-child-per-family policy doesn't allow it. We wouldn't even be able to send our own kids to nursery and no one wants to damage their own children's prospects. Eventually we had to stop people abandoning babies here. I'm not going to lie to you, we hired night-watchmen to patrol the entrance, and only allowed people in for treatment once they'd registered at the gate. And no one is allowed to hang around outside either.' The nurse sighed: 'Girl babies have never been given much of a future in a society that only values boys.'

It was not long before the doctor came out to tell me that the little girl was very strong. She had suffered some frostnip, but was otherwise completely healthy. He suggested that they keep her under observation for a day or two because newborns who got too cold were at risk of developing pneumonia. He did not say a word about birth permits or medical fees. And so the baby was taken to the Emergency Medical Unit. When I got to the radio station, my bicycle was already in the compound. The receptionist gave me the bicycle key and said, 'The man will be back to see you at nine o'clock.'

As that night's programme began, I dropped the usual round-up of news. Instead, I felt I had to tell my listeners about the shattering events of that morning, and to ask them to try and find the baby's mother and family. When we were half-way through, the producer told me I had an urgent phone call. In those days, there were no phone-in programmes. Listeners did not have their own phones, and only a very few ever called the producer's office and left messages to be broadcast on the programme. I could hear from the producer's voice that this was an unusual phone call, otherwise she would not have allowed me to be interrupted. My thoughts turned instinctively to my son: 'Has something happened to Panpan?'

'It wasn't a call from home,' the producer reassured me. 'It was a woman in tears begging you to speak to her.' It was clear the caller had aroused her sympathies.

I took the receiver. I could hear a radio playing what sounded like my programme music in the background.

'Hello, I'm . . .' I began but was interrupted by a tearful voice, saying urgently:

'I know you're Xinran, thank you. I'm listening to your programme at a corner shop. But I'm running out of money! Thank you for picking up my daughter, poor little girl. Thank you! Please kiss her for me, wrap her up warm . . .'

This was the child's mother! I asked anxiously, 'Where are you? Your daughter's at –'

'I know where she is, I followed you this morning. I know you took my baby girl to hospital. Thank you. Ai-ya . . . My money's running out. Tell my baby, I'm so sorry, I'm so . . . so . . .' And with a click, the anguished words were cut off and the line went dead.

I sat there dumbly, her sobs echoing in my ears, and an image of the child's little face, blue with cold, floating before my eyes.

The producer had her wits about her – she took the receiver from me and pressed the recall button. There was no reply. 'It must have been a public phone. I should have called her back straight away,' she said regretfully.

Dazed, I made my way back to the microphone. I simply did not know what to say. Then something made me pick this song to play: 'Let me dry your tears with my gentle hands, and warm your heart with my love . . .'

After that, I used to sing that song to myself for mothers who had lost their daughters. Some time later, when I was in London and set up my charity for adopted children, The Mothers' Bridge of Love, it was that song that we used as theme music on the

MBL website. I talked to the man who wrote the song, Guo Feng. In a phone call from China, he was sympathetic: 'Go ahead and use it if you like,' he told me. 'If that song can tell children that their birth mothers miss them, then that's my contribution to helping those mothers.'

After the programme finished that day, I put through a call to the Paediatric Department of the hospital. 'The baby's feeding well,' the doctor told me. 'She's sleeping peacefully now . . . But where is her mother? I haven't seen her.'

The next morning I went to the hospital to see the baby. Her bright little eyes were open, her face was pink now and she was no longer struggling and twitching. The doctor gave me a piece of blue-and-white patterned cloth and I recognised it as the material in which the baby had been swaddled. It was the only thing that had followed her into her new life. 'She's only two days old,' the doctor told me. 'She has a bit of a chest infection, but she was born lucky. You brought her here. A couple of days' observation and we can return her to her mother.' I took the cloth with one hand, and with the other, pushed a large envelope into his. It held money, he would have known that straight away.

But he pushed it back at me. 'There's no need. We are parents too, and we really take something like this to heart. We'll share the cost of caring for her between us!'

'I can't let you pay for her care. You're breaking the law as it is, just by rescuing and caring for her. You can't be expected to pay out for it too –'

But he cut me short with a dismissive gesture: 'We have plenty of wealthy patients. Let them pay a bit extra to cover her medical care.'

At this, I stopped arguing. Why shouldn't those corrupt officials fund her care? In a sick society, why not use underhand methods to fight back!

My bicycle tyre had been punctured by glass in the road, and that lunchtime I wheeled it down to a cycle repair stand I knew nearby. Of the 2,000 or so people who worked at the radio station, around 1,800 rode bicycles to and from work, and more than half knew the woman who ran this particular stand. This was not just because it was nearby, and the service cheap, fast and good, but also because she could mend anything, from footballs to rubber shoes and umbrellas.

I remember joking with her once: 'Your repairs are so good, and last so long, that soon no one will have anything for you to mend. Then you'll be out of a job, won't you?!'

'I do the sums differently,' she said. 'With more than a thousand of you at the radio station, if everyone comes for a repair just once a year, then that keeps me going for the whole year. That's without counting all the main roads and side streets around here. So many people rely on their bicycles to get to work. It just takes one person in a hundred to pass the word around about how good my work is and I'll always be in business. Of course, if one person said something bad about me, then I'd have to up and leave, because as you know, "bad news travels fast, good news stays at home". But I like it here. You're all educated people, and very kind to me. Every New Year, you give me presents of clothes. I know they're old and tatty to you, but I'm just an old cycle repair woman, I couldn't dream of buying these nice things for myself!'

As soon as I arrived, she carefully put down the umbrella she was mending and without waiting for me to speak, took my bicycle from me and pressed down on the front and rear tyres.

'The rear inner tube is punctured, and the front inner isn't too good either. Leave it with me, and after I've shut this evening, I'll bring it back to you and leave it at Reception. That way, you don't need to hang around waiting for me to repair it. Just don't forget to come and pay me tomorrow.'

'I've got nothing on this afternoon. Let me watch you change the inner tube, then I can learn how to do it.'

'Really?' She looked at me disbelievingly over her spectacles.

'Really, unless it's going to take me more than half a day. I wouldn't want to drag myself away when I'd only learned half the job.' I followed her over to a piece of ground, where she propped the bicycle upside down.

'All my handiwork is "ten-minute technology", you won't need a moment more. Tell me, what do you want to learn?'

'How to repair my bicycle. We can start when you've finished what you're doing.' I pointed to the umbrella she had put down.

'That needn't stop us. The woman didn't want it so she gave it to me to use for spare parts. I know I can fix it, and I will when I've got a spare moment. Come over here!'

She removed the valve core, pulled the valve casing up through the wheel rim and in one movement pulled out the inner tube using a piece of wood wrapped in a scrap of material.

'What have you been talking about on the radio lately?' she asked as she worked.

As she checked the inners, which were in a bowl of soapy water, for damage, I told her what I had talked about in my recent broadcasts. When I got to the events of the previous day and the abandoned baby, the repair woman suddenly paused in her work:

'Did you keep the blue-and-white cloth she was swaddled in?'

'Yes. Why?' I was surprised at her seizing on that small detail. I had thought she was just making conversation while we worked.

'There's probably a story attached to it, don't you think?'

'What do you mean?'

'I'll tell you something. Before I came to the city in 1987, I was a travelling midwife, but I gave it up because I became long-sighted and my hands started shaking, and I was afraid of harming someone.'

I looked astonished.

'I don't look like one, do I? I can tell you, babies are a lot more difficult than mending bicycles, umbrellas, footballs and shoes. Honestly, if you know what you're doing, you can have someone standing on their own feet and looking after themselves for fifty years. And if you're no good? You can kill a healthy person off in less than three days, especially when a woman gives birth. In childbirth, it's hard to avoid a haemorrhage. And puerperal bleeding is dangerous, it does a woman in, it's "tired blood". If a woman loses fresh blood, then she loses strength. Once she starts losing good blood, then she loses all her energy and that's when you get problems, anywhere in her body . . .'

Her words made me think of the many listeners' letters describing midwives – some were beneficent saviours, others were butchers and robbers. 'So did you "do" girl babies for people?'

I asked carefully, using the country euphemism, not daring to use the chilling word 'smother'.

The cycle repair woman had been rubbing down the puncture area on the inner tube. Now she paused in her work. 'I earned my living as a midwife, delivering the male heir into the world . . .'

I did not understand. 'Did you know if it was a girl or a boy before it was born?'

'Of course I couldn't know for certain. In those days, we didn't have ultrasounds and things like that. But if I looked at the woman's belly shape, belly button, and the expression on her face, then I could take a pretty good guess and get it right most of the time.'

'How could you tell?' I suddenly remembered my work colleagues gesticulating at my belly as they tried to predict whether Panpan would be a boy or a girl.

'You may think it's extraordinary but it's really quite straight-forward: when the belly sticks out in front, it's usually a boy. If the woman carries it more towards the back, it's usually a girl. A sticking-out belly button means a boy, a sticking-in one means a girl. And we had a saying where we lived, that a boy baby "eats" his mother up, but a girl is like face-paint. That means, women who are carrying girls look fresh and bright-eyed, but being pregnant with a boy has a much bigger effect on the woman.'

I was interested in these old wives' tales. 'Were there many people where you lived who knew as much as you about this?'

'I don't know. Probably not many. If everyone knew, then where would my dinners have come from?!'

'I'm not sure I understand.' By now I was confused about what this 'natural lore' meant.

'Before the baby was delivered, the family often used to ask me if it was a girl or a boy. Partly this was so they could get my fee ready, and also so they could prepare the birth celebrations. That was when it was a boy, of course. There were red-dyed boiled eggs to give to friends and family, celebratory couplets to burn, to tell the ancestors the good news and to thank the spirits for their kindness. And then there were the baby clothes to get ready, and . . .'

The bicycle mender stopped, looked up at the sky and went on: 'Something to do the evil deed. They would need things to put it out of the way.'

'What "things to put it out of the way"?'

'That was for when a girl baby was born,' she said with obvious reluctance. Then she changed the subject. 'It was just business sense. If you knew how to get the quote right, you could eat well all year round. If not, you lived off sweet potatoes for ten months in twelve.'

'A quote for delivering the baby?'

'If I could see it was going to be a boy, and it was the first-born, then it was an "incense birth".* I could quote three times the normal rate for that. If the mother was the wife of the eldest son, the birth was very auspicious because it continued the family line, and then it was six times. If it was neither of these, but still a boy, I could still ask for quite a good fee.'

'What if you could see it was a girl?'

'Well, first you had to find out what the family wanted. If they wanted the baby, even if it was a girl, then you quoted an ordinary fee, but if they wanted it put out of the way, you charged sky-high!'

'So what do you mean "put out of the way"?' We were back to my original question.

'Do you really want to know? You won't hate me for it, or broadcast my name?'

'Let's say that if I do put it into my programme, I'll just say I did my research and found out about it, but I won't mention your name or family name.'

'Okay, I understand. The programmes you make are a real help to women. So, I'll tell you . . . "putting it out of the way" means making sure, one way or another, that the baby won't live.'

'What? Isn't that killing her?'

'Well, I can't help it if you must use city folk's language so, yes, that's what it was.'

---

* Meaning the family now had an heir who would burn incense to the ancestors. (*Trans.*)

'And what kind of methods did you use?'

'Oh, all sorts! Twisting the umbilical cord twice round the neck, then as soon as the head came out, you could strangle it. If it came out head upwards, you could make it choke on the amniotic fluid, and then the baby couldn't even take one breath. Or you could put the baby in a basin, hold wet "horse-dung"* paper over its face, and in a few seconds its legs would stop kicking. And for women who'd never had a baby boy, just girl after girl after girl until the family were fed up with it, it was simple enough to chuck it in the slops pail . . . All sorts of ways, but I don't want to talk about it any more, it was so upsetting . . . a perfectly good little baby, not even allowing the mother one look, just dispatching it to the Underworld . . .'

Listening to this sent chills down my spine, and in my mind's eye I saw that little, twitching foot poking out of the slop pail in the Yimeng Mountain village again. I could hardly bring myself to imagine it. I could also hardly believe that so many tiny babies had died at the hands of this kindly woman before me – how many? I did not dare to ask . . .

Seeing me standing there looking stunned, she said helplessly, 'I was also ridding the family of a calamity.'

'These baby girls were a calamity?'

'Of course, you wouldn't agree, but we country folk were terrified the first child would be a girl. If it was, it meant that for a whole generation, or even several generations, the family wouldn't be able to hold up their heads in the village! What's that if not a calamity? Besides, if you had a girl baby, you wouldn't get even a scrap of land allocated, and you had one more mouth to feed. Then when she was grown up, you had to pay for the marriage clothes. It was a disaster all the way. Country people are raised in the mud, they don't get education or the kind of lives that city women have!'

'So was it always straightforward when you did it, then?' I felt she would understand what I meant by 'straightforward'.

'Of course not, I'm a woman too, aren't I? Sometimes I could

---

* 'Horse-dung' paper was a cheap, rough paper, made from plants and yellow-brown in colour. (*Trans.*)

see the mother was a good-looker, and I thought how pretty the baby would have been too, and I felt really sorry. Sometimes, the mum and dad would slip me a couple of coins behind their parents' back to take the baby away alive. One mother-in-law was really vicious and stuffed the "horse-dung" paper into the baby's nostrils with her own fingernails, but I knew right from wrong . . . I told her to give it to me to "send it on its way to the Underworld", and I wrapped the baby in the paper and took it with me. When I was far enough away, I unwrapped the baby, and it was still breathing!'

'Where did you take the babies to?'

'Some of them were lucky, if someone had ordered one from me in advance. Especially if a woman in town could not have children, the family often bought a baby from a midwife. If it wasn't out of my way, I might drop the baby at an orphanage, or simply leave it outside the gate of the county hospital for someone to pick up and take away. In those days, quite a lot of people would pick up girls that way. Mostly they would be sold to families in poor mountain villages where they were reared and then married to the son of the family. Life is hard for women; no dynasty or government values them. Anyway, that's enough of that. You put that piece of blue-and-white cloth away . . .'

I nodded, in silence. As I watched the repair woman running her hands over the rim tape around the inside of the wheel, I seemed to see lots of small pink babies being 'put out of the way'. I felt giddy and terribly distressed: for the mothers who had been unable to hold their daughters in their arms, for those baby girls who would never know who their mothers were, or had not even had time to open their eyes on the world!

'Do you have a daughter?' After a long silence, I asked her.

'I gave them all away.'

'Do you miss them?'

'Of course I miss them!' She looked at me fiercely. This was a side of the repair woman I had never seen before.

*

The next day, my colleagues told me that the bicycle repair woman had not set up her stall, and a week later she had still not re-appeared. She was gone, taking with her memories that would not fade. I had reopened old wounds, and I had the feeling she did not want to see me again.

4

The Dish-washer Who Twice Tried to Kill Herself

'This is not a story in a book, this is a serious responsibility . . .
This time she's got to go, I'm not going to be a good woman any
more.'

'WHY? WHY do you keep taking the easy way out? Didn't we agree that you'd talk about your problems, so we could all help you with them?'

Kumei ('Poor Little Sister')* had regained consciousness. She gazed vacantly in front of her, her eyes filled with anguish, but my exasperation had been simmering for so long that I could not hold back the angry words.

This was the second time she had ended up in hospital after trying, and failing, to kill herself.

*

Kumei did the washing-up at the Tiny Home Chef. This was a small family-run restaurant with just four tables each seating two people, two streets away from the second radio station where I

---

* *Ku* (suffering or hardship) and *mei* (little sister, young woman) indicates that she
both suffers and brings bad luck. But it is a nickname rather than a proper name: she
lost her original family names, both surname and given name, because her parents sold
her. (*Trans.*)

worked now in Nanjing. The husband did the cooking, while the wife shopped, looked after the customers, and took the money. Kumei prepared the vegetables, washed up and swept and cleaned. The café was at the front of the couple's house, in what I guessed must originally have been their sitting room, and was separated from the rest of the house by a narrow, dark passage piled high with supplies. The 'kitchen', constructed out of three pieces of sheet iron, was out in the back yard. Just a decade earlier, one glance inside the kitchens of family cafés like this would have ensured that you never swallowed another mouthful of their dinners again, in spite of the mouth-watering smells and sputtering sounds. But the Tiny Home Chef was clean and neat. Indeed it was so well organised that, even when the cooking was at its fiercest, and smoke and flames rose from the stove, you could stand there exchanging a few words with the cook or his wife without feeling overcome by the smells or in the way.

Minguang, the wife, was something exceptional in this sort of service sector business – a woman who collected second-hand books. She often provided book reviews for my programmes, so after they opened their little restaurant near my work, we began to see a lot of each other. I used to take refuge there from my busy, noisy office at lunchtimes and order a dish of stir-fried pork kidneys and bean sprouts or quick-fried tripe in soy sauce, accompanied by stir-fried seasonal greens and a bowl of rice. At two or three yuan for the lot, it was excellent value for money as well as being delicious.

While I was waiting for my food, I would open a book and drink a cup of green tea, or talk to Minguang about new books and authors. (She always had titbits of news and gossip for me, of the sort that never reached us in the official media, about books which had been censored or banned.) As I ate an appetising lunch, I could eavesdrop on my fellow diners' gossip . . . It was almost as if a play was being put on in front of me. I have always believed that such everyday street scenes enliven and inspire great works of art.

Most of the Tiny Home Chef's customers were regulars who, over time, had become friends. Many were bookworms too, drawn here because the manageress loved reading. We were self-contained, perhaps because people who read a lot tend to cherish their own personal space. It was rare for customers to share their dinners or to talk endlessly on their mobiles like most Chinese. Instead, when we met at the restaurant, we might exchange a few words about our families or books. Then we would eat our food, put down our chopsticks, pay the bill and say goodbye. At first, Minguang and I had little to do with each other, apart from when she contributed to my programmes and I ate lunch at her restaurant. It was only when she hired Kumei that we had something far more momentous to talk about.

Kumei had been introduced to Minguang by a niece, Ying, from Anhui province. Ying said that she was a quiet girl, whose husband had gone off to be a migrant worker and had never come back. Rumour had it that he had found himself a mistress in the city. Whether or not this was true, Kumei continued to slave away for her parents-in-law at home. They, on the other hand, did not stick up for their daughter-in-law, and even went around telling everyone that their son had found himself a big-hipped woman who had given them a grandson, while Kumei stayed at home eating up their insufficient grain rations! In these poverty-stricken villages, not having sons or grandsons was more serious than not having a house or land. According to Ying, everyone knew that Kumei had been pregnant, but none of the babies had survived. She had not been able to give the family an heir. This was apparently the reason why the husband had gone south in search of work.

Kumei had been bought as a bride from some distant village, and had no family or friends to defend her. She was illiterate, had no ideas of her own, and effectively lived like a beast of burden, slaving away all day and all night too. When Ying returned home for the Spring Festival, she was really upset by the pitiable state Kumei was in and so, when she got back to town, she hunted high and low for a job for her. Finally she heard that the Tiny Home Chef needed someone to help out, and in 1992 Kumei arrived.

Minguang and her husband had no spare room for Kumei, and the girl had to sleep in the restaurant. (In those days, it was almost unheard-of for city restaurant owners to provide their workers with proper accommodation.) A traditional southern-style coal brazier provided warmth in winter; no one worried about poisonous fumes, because as soon as you opened the door to the kitchen area, the draughts came howling through. At the height of summer there was also an old-style electric fan which thundered and shook, but was actually very little use in the Nanjing heat, which frequently reached 40°C.

Kumei started washing and chopping vegetables at half past ten in the morning, and worked on until half past ten at night, when she swept up and shut the door. However, local families sometimes rented the café for weddings or funerals, or birthday parties for the old folks or children, and in any case Nanjing was so hot in the summer that people often went out to snack and gossip until late at night, so it was often after midnight before Kumei got to bed.

From Monday to Friday every week I finished my programme at midnight, so on summer nights I often used to slip into the Tiny Home Chef if there were still customers, and have a refreshing bowl of cold noodles or some iced green tea. But unlike my fellow Nanjingers, I very rarely sat over a dish of whelks, chewing and chatting away with friends until the small hours. I could be anonymous here and that was what I wanted. Here I had my own space, free from the endless petty responsibilities that got me down in my working life.

It was one night in high summer that Kumei tried to kill herself for the first time.

In the building where I worked, the mains electricity was shut off at night so the air conditioning stopped too, except in my broadcasting studio where the temperature was controlled around the clock. The building's doors and windows were closed too, to keep the wind and rain out, so when I emerged from the studio the stifling heat and humidity almost overwhelmed me.

I decided to go to the Tiny Home Chef where I could have a snack and where it would be cool. I also needed to clear my head, always in a whirl after my programme, otherwise I would spend all night awake with no one but the stars to talk to. By that time, I had a motorbike – I was one of the first women in China to ride one. I cut the engine as I turned into the side street, not wanting to disturb the neighbours.

All the lights were on at the Tiny Home Chef, which was very unusual – I supposed there must have been a family party that evening, and it had just finished. Normally when that happened, the café was closed to other customers. I was disappointed, and was just turning the motorbike around when Minguang appeared in the doorway and called quietly.

'Xinran! Please come in.'

'I don't want to bother you. You get to bed,' I said still manoeuvring the motorbike round to show that I meant what I said and was not just being polite.

'Something's happened!' She sounded panicky.

'What's happened?' I turned the motorbike again and pushed it over to her door.

'Please come in. I'm so scared, and I was just thinking you might drop by for a chat. Let me get you some iced mung bean soup.' She did not wait for me to say yes or no, but went straight through to the kitchen.

There had obviously been a birthday party at the restaurant – for a little girl. Everything was pink, and bits of coloured paper decorations lay scattered across the food leftovers on the tables. Minguang's husband was silently clearing up. I had had very little to do with him; he had never given me any opportunity to chat. The most I ever got from him by way of an answer to my questions was a brief 'yes', 'there's some left', 'we had some' or 'don't know'. Then it was 'thank you' and 'goodbye'!

Minguang was soon back with a bowl of iced mung bean soup. 'I put two sugar lumps in it. That will cool you down!'

'What's happened to Kumei? Has she got the day off?' I asked casually, taking the soup from her. 'The party must have gone on really late. It's nearly half past one and you two are still clearing up. It's hard work running a restaurant, isn't it?'

'Kumei's been taken to Accident and Emergency! My niece Ying is with her.' Minguang gave a sigh, and distractedly lit a cigarette.

The soup spoon was half-way to my mouth. Now I put it down again and stared at her. 'But why? What happened?'

'She tried to kill herself . . .' Minguang said reluctantly, blowing out a smoke ring.

'Kill herself? Here? Today? Why on earth?' I felt a chill run through me. In response to my questions, Minguang's husband stopped clearing up and sat down. Twisting his hands together nervously, he said, 'We don't know.'

'But how did it happen? Have you told the police?'

'We don't know anything,' said Minguang. 'What have we got to tell the police? Before the birthday party she was fine, going about her work without any fuss and bother. She even said how sweet the birthday girl was. But when they cut the birthday cake, she just stood there in the corner, as if she'd forgotten what she was doing. I thought it was because she was from the country and had never seen a city birthday party, so I let her have a good look. Then she would know what to do next time there was a birthday party.

'I didn't think any more of it. But when the guests left, she disappeared too. I found her slumped over the boxes in the passageway. She was vomiting white froth and having convulsions. She seemed confused. I asked her what was up, but she wouldn't say. Eventually I was so worried, I shouted at her and turned her over. Underneath her there were two bottles, one of caustic soda, which we use for cleaning the tripe. The other was washing-up liquid. I suddenly realised she had swallowed the lot, and must have been trying to kill herself.

'We were both scared to death, so we called the emergency services. They told us the ambulance couldn't get into our alley, so my husband carried her on his back up to the main road. He almost couldn't get her accepted, as he didn't have enough cash with him! Damned hospitals nowadays, who do they think they are! Whatever happened to a doctor's vocation? Someone's sick and hasn't got any money? Forget it! They won't even let them through the door, let alone treat them!

'Anyway, enough of that. I sent a message to Ying on the pager. Her boyfriend runs a restaurant too, so they have cash in hand in the evenings, and luckily she went straight there. The doctors said Kumei had not swallowed a fatal dose, as it wasn't very concentrated – the washing-up liquid mixed in with the caustic soda had diluted its strength and her life was not in danger. But her stomach lining might be damaged. They would pump her stomach and then she could go home, but she would just have to be careful about what she ate from now on. We were worried something else might be wrong with her, so we made them keep her in overnight. Then the day-shift doctors could check her over and tell us if she could go.

'The whole business was terrifying! So why should we report it to the police? We have no idea why she did it. Don't you think the sight of a police uniform might give her even more of a fright? Country folk get scared at the sight of anyone smartly dressed in the city, and if they see a uniform they automatically assume it's the police. Like Kumei, for instance – one day two security men who guard the bikes for a local company came in, and she hid in the kitchen and refused to come out. She thought they were coming to get her.'

I felt that Kumei must have had a guilty conscience about something, and pursued my questions. 'So you didn't get her registered for a temporary residence permit?' At that, Minguang's husband looked at his wife, then got up and carried the dirty things out of the room.

Looking at her husband's retreating back, Minguang said: 'He said I should do that too! I had a good shout at him about it. It was just going to be an extra expense for our restaurant. You think doing everything by the book is so easy? You must be joking! It's not clear how to do it or what documents Kumei needs. Never mind having to spend money on getting people to sort it out, where do you actually go to do it? Back home in the countryside, she never even got one of those red-letterheaded certificates.* She's just got a bit of paper with the seal of the local tax office, and I reckon they were all illiterate too and didn't know what seal was used for what. They probably just gave it to her to get rid of her. My niece hasn't been any help sorting it out either.

'And here's another thing: even if, against all the odds, you do manage to get her registered, who's to say that she won't just up and go one day? Cases like that are never in the national news, but the locals are full of them. Lots of workers just quietly

---

* Legal and government letters always have a red letterhead. (*Trans.*)

slip away and disappear. If you fall out with them, they might take your belongings with them, or get their friends in to beat you up.

'You can't see inside someone's heart. If Kumei's got something she's bottling up, she hasn't told us about it. She never says anything, except "Thank you, Uncle and Auntie, you've been so good to me." If we've been so good to her, then why does she go and frighten us like this?' And Minguang lit another cigarette from the stub of the last one.

I watched her husband going back and forth, carrying the dirty dishes and the rubbish, and said, 'Let me give you a hand. It'll be cleared away in no time, and then you can go and get some rest.'

'No, no, put those plates down! We can't have you getting your hands dirty! Right then, when you've drunk your soup, off you go home. Your son will be waiting for you.' And Minguang stubbed out the cigarette she had just lit, produced an apron from somewhere, put it on and said, 'We're fast workers. We'll have these four tables done by the time you've finished.'

She was absolutely right. By the time I could see the bottom of my soup bowl, the pair of them had the little room clean and ready for reopening the next day, although I imagined the kitchen was piled high with dirty dishes. As I said goodbye, I thought that they were not going to get any sleep that night.

It was half past two in the morning before I got home. My three-and-a-half-year-old son Panpan was asleep, his face covered in sweat; my young *a-yi*,* Fen, sat at the window waving a fan. She looked concerned as she said, 'How come you're so late back, Sister Xinran? Surely the listeners didn't keep you at work talking about their problems?'

'No, just let me take a shower and I'll tell you, right? It's so hot in the flat. Why haven't you got the air conditioning on?'

'I can put up with it, and Panpan's little: once he's asleep it doesn't bother him. We save a bit of money that way, so you don't have to work away all hours on your programmes, your writing and your teaching.'

---

* An *a-yi* is a housemaid/nanny. (*Trans.*)

'Silly girl, saving money doesn't save lives. Isn't it better for you to get a few hours' good sleep and feel really well the next day?' I lectured her as I got my pyjamas ready to put on.

'You can use your education to earn money. I'm not clever enough for that, I can only earn money with my hands and feet. If I can save money for you, then a bit of sweat is just part of the work I do!'

The truth is, I thought to myself as I showered, all we learn from a few years' schooling is how to make a living buying and selling. It's all far more primitive and less worthy than the work these young women migrant workers do. They spend their time trying to save money for us, all out of the goodness of their hearts. Sadly, their honesty and good intentions are hardly ever acknowledged or appreciated.

Fen had been with us for eighteen months. I had hired her from the labour exchange. Like Kumei, she had a heart-breaking story to tell: she had only been married three months when the small, thatched cottage she and her husband lived in was compulsorily purchased by the government to make way for the Shanghai–Nanjing Expressway. They never received the money for their house and land, and so the couple were left with nowhere to live and no way of making a living.

By this time Fen was eight months pregnant and getting thinner every day. In desperation, her husband broke into the supplies depot and stole twenty eggs and two kilos of sweet potatoes. Unluckily for him, that very night a group of professional thieves also broke into the supplies depot, and the next day the Public Security Bureau put up a sternly worded notice urging the thieves to give themselves up. The poor man was so frightened that he did as he was told and turned himself in. The police knew perfectly well that he could not have taken a whole warehouse full of goods because he had no accomplice, but they triumphantly announced they had cracked the case and that this was the 'bandit chief'. He was sentenced to twenty-four years in prison, leaving Fen and a baby son of just a month old. Fen actually took the baby to the county town and asked if she could show her husband his newly born son, but permission was refused.

Fen had no choice but to go to her husband's parents and beg for help. The old couple said that they would bring up the baby, because he was their grandson after all. But they could not take her in and support her for the next twenty-four years. Fen was furious at such unjust treatment. She went straight off and spent the few cents she had put by for emergencies on a migrant worker's card and the cheapest bus ticket to Nanjing. When I saw her, she was chewing on a piece of dry bread, and the determined manner in which she was doing it convinced me she would be a good person to help around the house. Workers hired from the labour exchange now had accident insurance too, so I took her home with me.

It was just as I expected: everything she knew how to do was done well, and what she did not know, she did her best to learn. Most importantly, she was a really good soul, so good that sometimes it embarrassed me. For instance, if she came to the radio station to talk to me, she would not think twice about picking up a smelly, sweaty tracksuit which a colleague had left lying on a chair, and taking it home to wash. Then she would get me to take it back to work and quietly put it back where it had been left. However, the owners of the tracksuits were furious: this country bumpkin would probably ruin brand-name sports wear which had cost them two months' wages by not following the washing instructions. I tried explaining this to her gently, but Fen could not understand their indignation. Her reaction was: 'Fairy godmothers never announce their good deeds in public. Your colleagues may complain, but they're happy about it really. How could they not be, when someone's helping them out? Don't listen to them, Sister Xinran, I know what I'm talking about.' Eventually, I had to tell her a little white lie – that security had been tightened, and relatives were no longer allowed to wander in and out of the radio station – to stop her coming in to do her good deeds.

That night, once I had showered, I told Fen in outline what had happened to me when I left work. Then I turned on the air conditioning and went to my room to sleep. Before Fen shut her bedroom door, I heard her mutter to herself, 'Oh dear, another woman who carries her burden of suffering around with her!'

The next day, I was sent to cover the case of a woman who had suffered severe abuse in a village some distance away. I was there for three days, and thoughts of Kumei were put to the back of my mind. Almost every week now I got listeners' letters or calls to the programme with similar reports of migrant worker women trying to kill themselves, but I had had little personal experience of such cases in Nanjing. I saw labourers from the countryside every day, of course. Simply dressed and weather-beaten, they lived almost literally on the streets, kept themselves to themselves and worked silently around the clock. They formed the lowest level of urban society. But the rest of us, and that included me, were so busy keeping up with the dramatic changes taking place in our lives, and in the world around us, that we ignored this mass of migrant workers and their precarious lives. It was only when something happened to put the spotlight on women like Kumei and Fen that the city's comfortably off residents began to actually 'see' people who had previously been invisible to them. They did not, however, always recognise the value of their existence.

It was more than a week before I went back to the Tiny Home Chef. Kumei gave me a wan smile and carried on silently with what she was doing. Minguang looked exhausted, and with a glance at the pale-faced girl, said quietly to me, 'Last night, I suddenly felt afraid, I don't know why, and slipped quietly down to see what she was doing. Heavens, I was only just in time. She was sitting in the dark drinking something from a plastic container. I shouted at her to stop and grabbed the container from her. When I turned on the light and saw her face, I was shocked. I've never seen such misery, I can't begin to describe it to you!

'I asked her what it was all about, but I couldn't get a word out of her. I sat with her for ages, but she just cried and cried and wouldn't talk! Eventually I was completely exhausted and I put a quilt on one of our tables and lay down on it, and somehow we got through the night together. I don't think she slept at all, she tossed and turned all night. This morning, I actually felt fed up with it all. If she won't tell me what it's about, then it's like she doesn't respect me, isn't it?

'I paged Ying and told her to come and take Kumei away, otherwise I'd fire her and pack her off to the labour exchange. Ying came over this afternoon, and the café was empty so she dragged Kumei off into a corner, and there was a lot of whispering. Finally, while we were getting ready to serve dinners, the two of them came over to where I was preparing the vegetables, and Kumei suddenly fell on her knees in front of me and said, "Please forgive me, please don't send me home!"

'I've never seen anything like it in my life . . . I pulled her up but I really didn't know what to say to her. Ying put in impatiently: "What Kumei means is, she's so upset about something that she just can't bear it, but it's nothing to do with you two. You've been really good to her, a thousand times better than her own family. Isn't that right, Kumei?" Kumei nodded vigorously, as if she was afraid I might not believe her.

'Ying had to get back to her restaurant to open up, and I had customers, so I didn't say anything more. We were incredibly busy tonight, and Kumei behaved as if nothing had happened – she was as quick on her feet and as helpful as she normally is. Twice my husband said to me: "Let's keep her, she's so good." Xinran, when I look at how pale and thin she is, I get a bad feeling about it all. I'd really like to keep her, but then I get scared again. Being good isn't easy! I think in a couple of days I'll have a look around for another girl. I definitely want a chatterbox because, even if we quarrel, at least she won't be like Kumei and keep me on tenterhooks because I never know if she's dead or alive!'

When I went home that day, I told Fen what Minguang had said. Fen had had a tough time of it herself, and she often helped me understand what was going on with people who had something on their mind but could not bring themselves to tell anyone about it.

When I had finished, Fen put one hand on her heart and made a helpless gesture with the other: 'Sister Xinran, you city folk will talk to each other about anything, but in the country we aren't like that. We don't go around laughing and talking loudly, especially not women, and especially one who hasn't had a son. If you can't produce a son and heir to carry on the family line, then even hell's too good a place for you! Even when you've had a son, if you live with your parents-in-law, you're still not supposed to speak. It's only when you get to be a mother-in-law yourself that you get a chance to speak out. Go and see for yourself . . . How many women kill themselves once they've become mothers-in-law? City folk all say that men and women are the same, but no one believes that in the countryside! Of course Kumei's not going to tell her boss what it's all about. She wouldn't dare. She thinks that Minguang will think she's mad and will want to get rid of her!

'None of us can read and write, so we're different. I've lived with you all this time, but when I hear you on the phone to your friends, and you're all chatting, I still don't understand you. Take ironing, for instance. We just put the washing out to dry and it hangs out smooth with the wind and the sun. Why you want to spend money on electricity and iron perfectly good clothes flat as a board, I don't know . . . Even tree bark has creases in it. It gives you something to look at and feel. A tree with a completely smooth trunk would be ugly, wouldn't it? It's the same with people's clothes, isn't it? Anyway, if you really want to know what's wrong with Kumei, if you want her to get it off her chest, then you have to make her believe that she's not stupid.'

I started to get my son's things ready for the next day. 'How can I make her trust me? If you were me, what would you do?' I asked her earnestly.

'What would I do? Work alongside her? Have her to stay with us for a few days? I really don't know . . .' Fen had been folding piles of clothes. Now she paused.

'Do you trust me?' As soon as the words were out of my mouth, I regretted them. Of course she would say that she did. I hurriedly added: 'Why do you trust me?'

'Well, you're happy to learn things from me, like when I taught you to make griddle cakes. I was so proud that I could do things that Sister Xinran couldn't do! Like when you asked me to teach you the song "Friends". I thought, a big radio station presenter can't even sing a song, that's such a pity! That's when I trusted you, when I taught you to do things.'

I had never realised what 'trust' meant up to that point, and I later put Fen's words to good use in my work. By becoming a 'student', I learned how the peasants talked and how they made things with their hands. I also got to hear what many women were really thinking.

Two weeks went by and I was back at the Tiny Home Chef. Kumei's cheeks were gradually turning from a sickly pallor back to pink, and Minguang did not mention any concerns about the girl to me. I thought Kumei had become absorbed into city life like countless other country women and, in so doing, had succeeded in leaving the pain of her past behind her. But one afternoon, I got a message from Minguang on the pager: 'Please, Xinran, come to the Emergency Department at the People's Hospital, I beg you!'

I knew it must be serious – Minguang was a tough woman, who did not 'beg' anyone unless she was absolutely desperate. I jumped on my motorbike and was there in half an hour. I found my friend pacing up and down beside a bed in which Kumei lay asleep, ashen-faced against the white sheets.

'Xinran! It's so good of you to come. Look! Look at this – she's been fine up to now, and then she tries to kill herself again! She doesn't want to leave, but she doesn't want to live here either! Why's she doing this to me? I can't take any more of these frights. This time she's got to go, I'm not going to be a good woman any more. Her local town doesn't have a single telephone, and Ying's not answering her pager. I don't know where that girl's got to!' Minguang seemed completely at a loss, and her words were full of helpless fear.

'When was she brought in?' I asked, wanting to be of some practical help.

'This morning I went out, to a writers' meeting. By noon, she was still not up, so my husband went to call her. He found her unconscious on the floor in a pool of vomit. He called the ambulance straight away, and then he got me back. Never mind the money it's costing us, every time it happens it's terrifying and I can't take it. I made my husband shut the restaurant. We'll keep it closed a couple of days, and then we'll see . . . We have to get to the bottom of this, otherwise . . .'

'Was there anything unusual about her last night?' I asked, trying to figure out the possible reason.

'She seemed fine. There was a birthday party in the café, and the birthday girl gave her a piece of cake too!'

Kumei slept on unawares, in what was probably the most comfortable bed she had ever lain on in her life. She seemed to be hovering somewhere between life and death.

I found the doctor on call, and she told me that Kumei would live, but had had serious gastric bleeding. Her stomach had obviously been damaged by the chemicals in the cleaning fluids she had ingested. 'Why did she do it?' she asked me.

'I don't know. Perhaps . . .' But the truth was that I could not even begin to guess why.

Kumei's anguish and Minguang's helplessness left me feeling really upset. It was nothing to do with whether or not she was educated. The fact was that if a woman chose to try and kill herself it must mean that she was facing terrible problems, and could not resolve them. I felt I really should try and help. I went to the public phone in the hospital and called Fen. Would she be willing to help me nurse Kumei at home? I asked her. 'Of course!' she said. 'You're always going off to help people in the country-side. This is my chance to help someone in the city.'

When I told Minguang my plan, she was so grateful she practically fell on her knees and kowtowed to me.

'Xinran, if you would take her into your home for a couple of days, and get your *a-yi* to look after her, I would be eternally grateful! But I won't mince my words. You do understand, don't you, that, once she's out of here, her fate will be in your hands, nothing to do with me any more? This is not a story in a book, this is a serious responsibility. Have you thought about that? If not, I'll just pay the fees here, and take her down to the labour exchange. That way, we won't get into such a pickle again. It's just impossible to do right by her. Think it through properly . . .'

'It's all right,' I stopped her. 'Let me give it a try. There are so many women's stories on my programme, and sometimes hearing something similar gives women hope, and a feeling that they're not all on their own and no one knows about them. And where there's hope, there's a way out! My *a-yi* had a horrendous life in the countryside when she was young. Maybe there'll be sympathy between them and that will help Kumei open up.'

At that moment, Kumei opened her eyes. She was by now so dehydrated that she seemed to be looking out at us from a waterless desert. She had cried till she had no tears left. That was when I could not helping asking her: '*Why?*'

Kumei made no sound, just shut her eyes miserably. But then she resolutely opened them again, sat up and started to get out of bed. Minguang and I were so startled that we did not try to stop her as she pulled the curtain back and put on her shoes. But then we grabbed her, one on each side, as she nearly fell to the floor.

'I'm going to call the doctor. If they say it's okay, then she can come home with me,' I said to Minguang and went to the duty doctor's office. Forty minutes later I returned with the discharge letter, to find Minguang and Kumei sitting silently on the edge of the bed.

Kumei was extremely anxious as we travelled home in the taxi. She had obviously never been in a car before, but luckily it was a short trip. When we arrived at the flat, Fen had put an extra folding single bed in her room and was just rearranging the furniture so that it looked as if the room had always been like that. I handed Kumei over to her and took a taxi back to the hospital for my motorbike. From there I went to the nursery to pick up Panpan. Once I had taken him home, I went back to the radio station to prepare that evening's *Words on the Night Breeze*. I called home twice during the evening, and Fen told me that Kumei was asleep.

When I returned home after the programme, I saw the two of them silhouetted at the window in the moonlight, apparently talking, and could not help feeling moved. They had clearly made friends – Kumei was saying something to Fen – and I left them alone, feeling that they needed more time on their own.

They must have gone to bed late, but they were up before me in the morning, and had done the housework almost without making a sound. Panpan was delighted that we had another *a-yi*, and the two of them had quietly managed to cajole him into getting dressed. I had always insisted on doing Panpan's break-fast. I was a firm believer that the starting-point for a good day was a pleasant and freshly made breakfast; it was really important for parents to make mornings a focus of family life, something that the child, especially one who never wanted to get up in the morning or go to bed at night, looked forward to. However, that day I decided to ask Kumei and Fen to make breakfast for Panpan and all of us. Seeing them working harmoniously together, I felt immensely grateful to Fen and I could see a gratifying change in Kumei.

The fourth day Kumei spent with us was a Friday, and when I arrived home from work in the evening, I told Kumei that I would not be going to the radio station on Saturday. We would do the housework together in the morning and in the afternoon we could all take Panpan to the park. If she wanted, I could arrange for Minguang and her husband to meet us there. Kumei gave Fen a serious look, and then nodded. It was exactly as Minguang had said: 'She's afraid I might not believe her.'

We sat together on the grass, and Fen took Panpan off to play. Before she left, she whispered something in Kumei's ear. Kumei again looked serious and nodded. Then she told the three of us – her employers and me – why she was so sad.

She was born in the mountains in western Hunan province, and had been sold as a bride to a family in Yuanyang, in North Anhui. The day after her arrival, she was forcibly married. The man was a brawny peasant who never said a word to anyone. Kumei was soon pregnant.

As her time grew near, her mother-in-law spent every day burning incense and making her devotions at the shrine, begging Guan Yin, the goddess of mercy, to bless the family with a grandson. Kumei went into labour and, that evening, because it was the first grandchild, the whole family gathered in the kitchen outside, waiting for news that Kumei had produced a baby boy. Kumei was terrified in case it was a girl. They would be so angry with her.

The midwife delivered the baby and, before it had uttered a cry, checked it by the pale light of the oil lamp. She gave a sigh. The disappointed parents-in-law and the rest of the family waiting outside cursed, and then departed one by one. The midwife said a few words, took her fee and left. Kumei did not know what to do. As her newborn struggled to draw her first breath, she tried to swaddle her, tears running down her face. Ever since she was a child, she had heard adults say that if the first grandchild was a girl, it would not be allowed to live. If it did, it 'broke' the family's 'roots'. The first surviving baby had to be a boy.

She looked at the bowl of water the midwife had prepared for her before the birth. This was the Killing Trouble water, for drowning the girl baby in. For a boy, the bowl for washing the baby was called Watering the Roots bath. She knew it was her duty to end her daughter's life by drowning her in the bowl, and this is what she did.

The next year, she got pregnant again and unfortunately gave birth to another girl. This time, her mother-in-law pulled the baby out of her hands and held it under the water in the basin. But the baby was determined to hang on to life, and when everyone but the husband had left, Kumei found she was still alive.

She begged her husband to take the baby to the city to give her a chance of life, but no one listened to her entreaties. For less than twenty-four hours she had felt what it might be like to be a mother, but had no dreams of how her child would grow to adulthood. Instead, all she knew was that she had committed an offence. She was the one who had failed to present the family with an heir. So when the husband went off to get work in the city and did not come back, she knew it was because of her. His thwarted parents wanted to get rid of her: she had brought misfortune on the family. Fortunately for her, Ying brought her to town. With Minguang and her husband, this girl, who had received nothing but harsh words and treatment since childhood, was not only treated kindly, she also earned the first money that she could call her own. She felt she must be in heaven!

But then she saw a five-year-old girl celebrating her birthday in the Tiny Home Chef. She was astonished. Was it possible that city folk really looked after girl children like this? She looked like a girl in a fairy tale. For the first time Kumei herself understood what it might have been like to be the mother of a little girl. If her daughters had lived, they could have been just as pink and adorable. If they had skirts like city girls, they would have been as pretty too! If only they had been able to come and see the city . . . but they'd never even had the chance to live for a day. She was overwhelmed with such bitterness that it finally drove her to despair, and to try to kill herself.

At least that way she might hold those small naked bodies in her arms once more.

When Kumei had finished, she asked us, weeping, 'Why couldn't my daughters have lived? Why did I have to kill my own daughters? I wish they could have had just a mouthful of that delicious birthday cake, just one mouthful! If only they could have put on those pretty clothes, just for a day!'

We sat in silence, with Kumei's words echoing in our ears. *Why couldn't my daughters have lived?*

Kumei carried on working at the Tiny Home Chef until I left China in 1997. Minguang turned Kumei's story into a novella which I read out on my programme. Among the many listeners' letters I received in response, a dozen were from women who told me that they too had lost their first daughter.

Later Minguang told me that the reason Kumei had swallowed cleaning fluids, including the washing-up liquid, was that, since she was illiterate, she thought that all cleaning products were the same as pesticides.

Countless numbers of country women in China commit suicide by swallowing pesticides. In a 2002 United Nations report, China came top of the list for female suicides, and pesticide was the favourite method. China is one of the few countries where more women than men commit suicide.*

---

* Suicide is China's fifth-biggest killer, with women most at risk. (BBC News China website, 04/2002). See Appendix C.

5

Extra-birth Guerrilla Troops: A Father on the Run

'She cries almost every night, and says she's been dreaming about the girls. I don't really believe it. We work so hard all day, we don't have time to dream!'

AN EXPRESSION which became popular in China in the 1990s was 'extra-birth guerrilla troops'. The term came from a sketch on the CCTV (the state TV channel) New Year's Party show in 1990 which featured a peasant couple who, after having had three daughters, leave home to escape the birth control regulations so that they can continue to try for a son. As they wander from place to place, they grumble and squabble with each other. The sketch took the government line in its depiction of the harm done by 'extra' births, but it also showed how hard the life of this 'floating' population was.

After that, the media gave the name 'extra-birth guerrilla troops' to couples who did a runner and went anywhere in China, often by train when they could, or even abroad so the woman could get pregnant and give birth away from their registered residence. As stories I uncovered proved, they moved more swiftly and fought more tenaciously than the soldiers of the Communist Red Army evading the encircling blockade of the Guomindang nationalist forces during the Long March.

I am sure that anyone passing through the outskirts of cities would have come across these 'guerrillas'. They were not ordinary street beggars, and were rarely seen in city centres; or if they were, they did not stay long. That was because the old ladies who ran the neighbourhood committees in every street and housing block kept everyone's behaviour under minute scrutiny. These old women had an unshakeable devotion to their social duties – they had fought for the 'good of the people and the glory of their country' since their revolutionary youth and nothing was going to deter them from continuing in the same old routine. Each morning they were up before it was light, wearing their red armbands and patrolling every corner of their jurisdiction. Their responsibilities ranged from helping the local police solve murders and robberies, right down to ensuring that passers-by were neatly dressed, and their bicycles were properly parked, and telling off adults for letting children eat cold snacks. In a word, there was almost nothing which did not fall within these old ladies' remit.

China had a very imperfect legal system before the 1990s, so just how did the central government of this vast country get its one billion citizens to obey orders with such docility? These ubiquitous local guardians of law and order must claim a large part of the credit! After the one-child policy was implemented, they kept an especially vigilant eye on people who had guests to stay in their homes. When a good friend of mine spent a couple of days with me in Nanjing on his way to take his child to visit the grandparents, they puffed and panted their way up the stairs to my flat on the fifth floor and demanded to know whether he had the certificate to prove that this was his only child!

The 'extra-birth guerrilla troops', however, had neither temporary city residence certificates, nor letters from their villages releasing them to get labouring jobs, nor single-child certificates. In big cities, they were right in the middle of government territory, behind enemy lines as it were. They could pass swiftly through but could not linger. Many of these intrepid 'guerrillas' were actually good people and courageous parents, who braved the city streets in the hopes of being able to leave their 'unplanned' daughters there. They were well aware that city folk lived much better than they did, and treated girls much better too. These guerrilla peasants did not have the heart to kill their girl babies as some more backward villagers did, but in keeping with the traditions and ignorance in which they had grown up, they still firmly believed that they needed a son or their lives would be blighted and they would not go to heaven. Their forebears in the Underworld would be angry with them for not producing a son to carry on the family line and they would never ever be able to rest in peace! These people were torn between the enlightened standards of modern civilisation and the cruelty of ancient tradition, where human feelings could lose their way.

They were also witnesses to the economic and political reforms which opened up China. Because of the time they spent wandering from place to place and crisscrossing the country by train in their guerrilla war with the authorities, they had first-hand experience of the way city and countryside were changing, and the increasing gap between rich and poor. No one understood the economic boom the way they did, just as no one else had their intimate knowledge of the legal loopholes and local government corruption that gave these peasant 'guerrillas' a space within which they could exist.

The first time I came across them was on the train from Zhengzhou to Chengdu. We were on the Longhai line,* the most northerly of the east–west trunk routes. China's rail system, developed in the 1950s, at first had three east–west routes and three north–south routes, and now has an additional two north–south routes. By the 1980s, the way passengers scrambled madly to get on a train and grab a seat made its shortcomings clear. Reporters like myself got privileges when we travelled and to other business travellers we were the 'fat cats', but actually China was so poor and backward that even with our privileges, work trips were desperately uncomfortable, a sort of 'foreign' or 'ocean' penance. (Business travel was regarded as something foreigners did, and as most of them arrived in China from the Pacific Ocean, the character 'yang' 洋 meaning 'ocean', came to be applied to people or things arriving in China from abroad, and simply meant 'foreign'.)

There was very little sleeping accommodation on trains, and

---

* Running a total of 1,736 km from Lianyungang in the east to Lanzhou in the northwest. (*Trans.*)

to get a bunk in a four-bed 'soft sleeper' compartment you had to be at least as senior as an army colonel or a city mayor. Local cadres from county towns or smaller townships were too junior to aspire to soft sleepers; the best they could wangle for themselves were 'hard sleepers'. Hard sleepers were a new arrangement, having been introduced with the reforms (rather like the old 'couchettes' on French trains, they had six hard bunks to a compartment, three on each side, top, middle and bottom, though no door).

The three of us reporters on the train that day were from different news units and were on our way to Chengdu to cover a national economics conference. We only had seats for the long journey – our status was still not enough to get us even hard sleepers. The rail staff who sold hard sleeper tickets were extremely arrogant, and in retrospect I think they were probably among the first government employees to work out how to use their position to feather their own nests, as the reforms kicked in. Of course, it is true that plenty of reporters have also used their privileges to make a bit extra on the side, otherwise they might have put a stop to the runaway levels of corruption in China today.

We got on the train and found our seats; the fourth seat was empty until a middle-aged man came along and took it. He was dressed in faded, old army fatigues, and was polite and un-assuming. He had no suitcase, only a cheap bag made of plastic which appeared to contain the sort of snacks most Chinese take on long journeys: flat bread, pickles and boiled eggs. He carried nothing else that would give a clue as to his job and back-ground.

It is the occupational disease of reporters to ask questions. The way I look at it, the chances that, in this vast world with its billions of inhabitants, you will sit next to a certain person are so remote that such chance encounters must be a matter of fate. A long journey is a great opportunity to get to know your fellow passengers, and I have always been endlessly curious. However, it was not I who put the first question, but one of my colleagues.

'Good evening. Where are you going?' he asked politely.

'Good evening,' the man responded. 'Are you all three travelling

together? You look like senior cadres.' This was a confident conver-
sation-opener.

'No, no. we're all reporters, one from a radio station, one from
a TV station and one from a magazine. What about you?'

'So you all work in the news. That's unusual. I really admire
people who work in the news. You show us which way things
are going, you live with the news every day. Your job must be so
interesting! So where are you all off to?' He was beginning to
sound like a reporter himself, I thought.

'To cover a meeting in Chengdu. What about you? From your
accent, you must be from the south.'

'Chengdu, eh? That's a fine place, such beautiful scenery. Plenty
of bargains to buy there. And as for the women, they're cleverer
than the men!'

'Really? Two of us have never been before, though Xinran has.
It sounds as if you've been there a lot.'

'Not that much, only once. I learned a bit about the place, like
the *18 Wonders of Chengdu*.'

'What are they?'

'I'll tell you about them. Actually, they keep changing with the
times.' And he began to recite in rhyming verse:

'1: *Chengdu people get sick if they don't go to a tea house
    every day.*
2: *Those clever Chengdu women are adorable.*
3: *Chengdu men love those beautiful women who bend
    their ears.*
4: *Chengdu people eat pickles at every meal.*
5: *Vendors of "gamblers' snacks" shout their wares every
    night.*
6: *There are mah-jong games on every street corner.*
7: *When a mouse dies, everyone gathers around to look.*
8: *Everyone rushes to sunbathe every time the sun comes
    out.*
9: *No one can beat the people of Chengdu at gossiping
    and bragging.*
10: *In Chengdu, guests get treated to a foot or a head
    massage.*

11:   *Small traders have the most carefree life.*
12:   *Even successful business people love their fly-blown cafés.*
13:   *People set up their chess games on every street corner.*
14:   *Chengdu young misses turn into young madams.*
15:   *All the women wear leather shoes.*
16:   *The more newspapers there are, the better they sell.*
17:   *Bicycles come with umbrellas over the seat.*
18:   *It's quicker to go to work by bicycle than by bus.'*

And then he continued: 'Pi County beans, Pi Tong liquor, Sichuan embroidery, garlic, Chuanxiong herbal medicine, Yunding Mountain ginseng, Da Hong Bao Sichuan pepper, red oranges and mandarins, hairy oranges, pork sausages, hot peppers, snow pears, navel oranges, yellow catfish ... these are all things that Chengdu is famous for.' Now he sounded like a tourist commercial for Chengdu (though in fact everywhere in China has its list of 'Wonders', and these are constantly changing).*

Our fellow passenger was clearly no fool: as he talked, we were struck by how adroitly he evaded our questions, again and again turning the conversation away from himself. What was he doing? From what he said, he seemed to have quite a bit of experience of the world. He did not seem like someone from the countryside wearing army fatigues as a fashion item, but on the other hand, with his weather-beaten face and smell of sweat, he could not have been a city or town worker either. I was intrigued, and spent the first part of the train journey trying to work out where this man was really from.

We had begun our journey at night, and the chatter and clamour amongst the passengers soon stilled. As the carriage grew quiet, my colleagues leaned their heads against the windows and nodded off. I, however, had a long-standing back problem, exacerbated by the hard train seats, and I had to keep shifting and changing my position. The man sitting opposite appeared to understand my discomfort and, without being asked, he kept his legs tucked away to allow me more space.

---

* See Appendix D for the full list of Chengdu 'Wonders'.

After about half an hour, he got up. I thought he must be going to the toilet, but to my surprise, he went in the other direction. As I watched him make his way carefully through the packed carriage, I was puzzled. The dining car had closed, the toilet was in the other direction: what was he doing? I guessed he must have a companion sitting in another compartment . . .

About half an hour later, he reappeared, bringing with him a little girl! She was only about eighteen months old, with huge eyes. She sat on his knee, as good as gold, sucking her thumb and looking intently across at me. Before I had time to say hello to her or ask who she was, the man said, 'This is my daughter. She was sitting with her mother, but I thought it was too crowded and those passengers are not as nice as you, so I brought her to sit with me. It'll give her mother a chance to have a bit of a nap too.'

I was impressed at how caring he was towards his wife – in all the listeners' letters I received, it was extremely rare to read about a man who was prepared to take care of the children. The little girl soon fell asleep in her father's arms.

The man kept stroking his little daughter's hands and feet as he held her. Watching him, I could not help reflecting bitterly on my own father. He had never tried to be a parent to me and so I had never known him. Nor did I even have many memories of this sort, of my mother. If she had ever petted or cuddled me, it must have been when I was too young to remember. I never grew up with either of them: the Great Leap Forward, the task of building up China's army and industry, and the Cultural Revolution had all, one after another, stolen my family from me. I have never even had a birthday with them. I had grown up in an era where one's country and the Revolution came before everything.

As all these memories went through my mind, I felt tears form in my eyes and threaten to roll down my cheeks . . . But I had no intention of letting anyone see me cry. I was brought up in the belief that crying is a sign of weakness. I was rubbing my face pretending that I'd just woken up, when the man got up and said in low tones, 'We're getting off soon. Goodbye.' 'Goodbye,' I whispered back.

The little girl had woken up and scrambled up on to her father's shoulder where she rested, sucking her thumb and looking at me with those big, bright eyes. I waved at her, and she extracted her thumb from her mouth and waved back: 'Goodbye'. I pressed my hand to my lips and blew her a kiss, and she imitated my gesture and blew one back. I tapped my nose with my thumb, and she did the same with her little thumb. I put both hands on top of my head and waggled them like a rabbit's ears, and she put her little hands on either side of her cheeks and waggled them too. I remember the last one we did before she disappeared: it was 'orchid' fingers,* my big 'orchid' against her small one!

The train drew into the station. It was a short stop – just three minutes. At that time of night, few passengers got on or off. I looked out as the train started to move, but could not see the man and his daughter among the small number who were leaving; I supposed they must be out of view on another part of the plat-form.

I kept trying to get into a comfortable position, and a kind-hearted colleague insisted that I swap places with her and sit by the window. It was much better – that way, I could lean against the window frame and take some of the pressure off my aching back. There was still the whiff of my fellow passengers' smelly feet, however, to keep me awake, and I rested my head against the window and looked out. It was pitch black outside, except for a few pricks of light. These, I knew, came from remote shacks which housed the track inspectors. They lived out there all year round and it was their job to check the points for stones which had rolled off the mountainside and might block the railway line.

Eventually, we arrived at Xi'an station. This was a big station, and the stop – fifteen minutes – was long enough to allow people to get off and buy more food and to stretch cramped limbs. I did not get out but just looked through the window; not far off there was a handcart with food on it, in front of which I could see a sea of hands. No one was queuing. It occurred to me that no amount of attempts to inculcate an altruistic Communist spirit

---

* Gesture in Chinese dancing: outstretched hand and fingers, with middle finger lowered in a circle to meet the thumb, like the petals of an orchid.

had managed to vanquish that capitalist belief in the need to put oneself and one's own interests first.

The train had begun to move again when I suddenly saw the little girl with whom I had been playing finger games sitting beside one of the carts. She was still sucking her thumb, and clutched a large steamed bun, or *mantou,* in the other hand. She stared blankly at the moving train; I could not see her father, but I pressed my face hard against the window pane and made 'orchid' fingers at her. It was only my way of saying goodbye to her again. I didn't think she could see me, even though the train was moving very slowly. Imagine my surprise when I realised she had seen me. She raised her little hand in the direction of the departing train and made 'orchid' fingers back. What a clever little thing!

The train picked up speed and once more plunged into the dark night. The memory of that adorable girl stayed with me. I was actually rather jealous of her parents; I had longed to have a daughter but sadly it was not to be. In fact, 'wanting' was not a word that even entered my dreams. I belonged to that genera-tion of Chinese whose lives had been marked by a series of crises: we had been born during the terrible famine of the Great Leap Forward; I started primary school in 1965, but in 1966 the Cultural Revolution shut almost every school and college; in 1975, when I should have been going to university, we were sent to the countryside to work; in the 1980s, when we should have been becoming mums and dads, the one-child policy was brought in; life was pretty hard until the economic reforms opened up China and then in the 1990s, unemployment hit . . .

Suddenly my thoughts were interrupted by the train's loud-speaker: 'Will Comrade Xinran, from the radio station, please come to the train controller's office in carriage 7 to take an urgent phone call!'

They were calling me. I was alarmed: had something happened to my son? But it could not be that. The radio station would not regard a private matter as so urgent. Was it a national emergency? Being a radio presenter carried greater political responsibilities than working in TV or the press because few people had TV and so many were illiterate. I remember being told this just after I had started the job; the station head talked to me about my choice of career and said that in the event of an attempt to overthrow the government, it was we radio broadcasters who would be in the front line because we were the mouthpiece of our rulers!

I rushed along to carriage 7. On my way, I thought I caught a glimpse of the man who had been sitting opposite me but dismissed the idea as ridiculous; after all, I had seen the little girl on the platform with my own eyes. How could her father still be on the train?

The train controller passed the phone to me: the gist of the message was that a news blackout had been imposed by central government. While Soviet leaders were visiting China, there was to be no mention in the media of reforms in the Soviet Union or of normalisation of Sino-Soviet relations. The restrictions were to apply to all news broadcasters for the next twenty-four hours. (No one anticipated the student demonstrations which greeted the Soviets' visit.)

By this time, I was used to urgent orders to 'tread carefully' with the news, but I could not help thinking they were making too much of it all. How could I broadcast international news while I was on a train? They could just have left a message for me at Chengdu Radio. In any case, Chengdu Radio reporters would surely have received the same order. It was a typical over-reaction by officials who needed to be seen to be carrying out their superiors' orders to the letter, because they were afraid they might lose their jobs. Nowadays young Chinese, let alone people in the rest of the world, have no idea that in imperial times no official of any level would dare to turn their back on the emperor, still less say 'no' to an order.

As I returned to my seat, squeezing my way through the crowded carriages, my mind was still on being a newscaster, and the difficulties of doing the job when faced with arbitrary restrictions.

Then, by some quirk of fate, I found myself almost face to face with the little girl's father! He was sitting next to a woman who was very pregnant, a holdall in his hand. When he saw me standing there in front of him, he looked terror-struck. We stared mutely at each other.

'What's happened to your daughter?'

'She –'

'She what?' Suddenly the penny dropped. I was aghast. Surely they could not have abandoned her at Xi'an station? But it was clear that his wife was expecting another baby, and if they already had a daughter, there would be nowhere for them to hide. The Family Planning Office would be after them and they would be dealt with severely. Had these parents really abandoned their little daughter at dead of night in a strange place? I hardly dared imagine . . .

I could see that the parents did not know what to say or do. I felt the blood rush to my face, and was on the point of yelling at them: 'How could you throw your own child out? She's so little, how's she going to survive? Have you thought about the terrors she's going to face from this moment onwards?' The man obviously saw the outburst that was coming, and stood up. He steered me forcefully towards the toilet at the end of the carriage and pushed me inside. Blocking the doorway, he said in a low voice, 'I beg you, comrade, please!'

'You . . . your own daughter – left on a station platform!' I spluttered, so indignant I was unable to get a coherent sentence out.

'Yes, I gave her a bun. The stall-holder will look after her.'

'Do you know the stall-holder?'

'No, I don't.'

'Then how can you possibly know she'll look after her? You're her father, don't you love her? What about her mother's feelings?' The words were no sooner out of my mouth than I remembered the way he had been petting his daughter.

He looked close to tears. 'She's our flesh and blood! Of course we love her. But the children were having a worse time on the run with us!' he said, swallowing hard.

'Children?! You mean you have more than one child?' I asked, unwilling to believe my ears.

'This one was the fourth girl, we . . .' His voice sank so low that I could hardly catch what he said.

So it was that in that train toilet I heard the story of 'extra-birth guerrillas' for the first time. It is a memory which still fills me with pain.

The man was from Jiangxi province, from a village ruled by a single clan. He was the eldest son of the family, the first of three brothers. Since his marriage, he and his wife had been constantly on the move. When his wife was three months pregnant, his parents told them they should move to town: that way, it would be easier for them to make a living. And if it did happen to be a girl, the people in the village would never know she had been born. The last thing his parents said before they left was: don't come home without a grandson! Don't humiliate us by leaving us without a son and heir to carry on the family line, was what they meant.

The man knew that if he and his wife had not produced a son within ten years, he would be stripped of the land and other benefits to which he was entitled as the eldest son, so he promised to bring them back a son; that way, his parents could hold their heads high and the clan would have a future. But the Good Lord had not listened to his daily prayers, and in seven and a half years his wife had had four daughters, one after the other.

Looking out of the window, he said flatly:

'We've been on the run for seven and a half years, we've travelled the length and breadth of China. Soon after the first girl was born, my wife got pregnant again. As she got bigger, people began to eye her up and say, "You're not thinking of having an 'extra birth', are you?" We had to keep moving on, in case the family planning officers caught us and forced her to abort a baby boy.'

'Didn't you say all four were daughters?'

'Yes, but each time we hoped it might be the boy we wanted!' he said, impatient with my lack of comprehension. This had not even occurred to me.

'But why do you need to abandon your daughters? Don't some people take their children with them as they keep moving?'

'Take the children with you? If it's not your first-born, then where would you go to have the baby? You can *buy* a birth permit – for tens of thousands of yuan – but where would we get money like that from? I'll never forget how terrified my eldest girl was when the family planning officers barged in to look for her mother! Her little legs were shaking like a leaf. If you go on the run with the child, you have to have the money to feed and clothe her as well as her mother. If her mother doesn't eat, the baby in her belly won't thrive, and if the mother does eat, what will the child eat?'

'If you have money for the rail fare, how come there's none for food?'

'It's not so simple. Please just hear me out. After the child-trafficker took our eldest daughter away, I was broken-hearted. And my wife cried for three months. When the second daughter was born, she had no milk. The baby nearly starved. We just managed to keep her alive by feeding her a little rice water,' the man said in a hoarse voice.

'When my wife got pregnant for the third time, we had a good talk and decided we had to take the second daughter to the city. At least there people were more educated and, who knows, she might end up with good folk!'

'But the one-child policy's so strict there, how did you manage not to get caught?'

'We can beat the devil at his own game, as the saying goes. I shouldn't say that, though, that's not really what I meant to say. What I mean is that on the outskirts of cities there are lots of places where you can stop and have a rest. Abandoned factories, old storage depots, the storage depots on building sites, where they're always looking for watchmen. The money isn't much but at least you don't have to sleep outdoors. My wife's a clever woman, she made a bit of money washing and mending for the migrant workers. Then when the baby was due, we told them we were going home for the birth. We bought the cheapest tickets and got as far away as possible, and went to some small town where no one knew us.'

'Don't they check the birth permit there?'

'They did ask, but you give them a bit more money. Besides, we're outsiders, they know we're not going to stay, so they just help with the birth.'

'How do you manage to find a doctor?'

'There are lots of people like us on the road. You soon learn the tricks. And you can find lists, stuck on the electricity poles at the side of rail tracks, of people willing to deliver babies and do abortions. They do a roaring trade in it nowadays, because everyone wants a son in the family.'

He was telling the truth, I knew: everything he said fitted with hints I had heard and the little research I had managed to do. You could find a profitable niche as a doctor in the gap which existed between the law and family custom. What I wanted to know about was what had happened to their daughters: 'So your daughters were all –'

He did not let me finish the sentence. 'Yes, they were. On the road or on the railroad, all over China, we left four daughters. The one you saw was the fourth. She was a good girl, and such a pretty little thing.' He was unable to go on . . .

'Aren't you worried what might have happened to them?'

'What's the point in worrying? If they're very lucky, they'll survive. If not . . . Girls are born to suffer. It's too bad they're not boys.'

'But what about your wife? She's a woman too, after all.'

'Yes, she can't handle it the way I do. She cries almost every night, and says she's been dreaming about the girls. I don't really believe it. We work so hard all day, we don't have time to dream!'

'Will you keep on running?'

'If I had a son, I'd go straight back home. I've managed to put a little money by, and even if we're starving, I won't break into those savings. I'm just longing for the day my wife gets it right!'

'And if she doesn't have a son?' I knew I was being cruel but it was a real possibility.

'What do you mean? I've still got two and a half years. And when it happens, then I'll go home and become head of the clan.'

'But your wife has suffered so much, physically and emotionally!'

'A woman who doesn't have a son has nothing to live for. I'm good to her! She may be miserable but I'm miserable too. If we had a son, I'd have some daughters too. I could look after them. Please leave my wife out of this, I beg you, and please don't report us! We'll get off the train straight away, okay?'

'You go where you want to go. I won't report you, for your four daughters' sake!'

As I made my way back to my seat, I had a good look at his

wife. Her face was lined and etched with pain, no doubt from the tears she had shed for her daughters. Men will never understand the emotional bond between a woman and the baby she carries in her womb for nine months. Every injury to that child is ten thousand times more painful to the mother than cutting flesh from her own body.

But I had to continue my journey. At the next station I think the man and his wife left the train and vanished into the crowd. What would happen to that mother, I wondered. If she gave birth to a fifth daughter, would she simply leave her baby at an anonymous station like this one, on a corner of the platform, in the toilets, or where? Now I had to pray for this woman to have a son before the daily suffering and the exhausting journeys killed her. If at last she had a son, presumably it would be lovingly swaddled, they would get back on the train and go home triumphantly to her husband's village. It was so hard to believe.

In my mind's eye, I often see the middle-aged man's fourth daughter, making her little 'orchid' fingers . . .

As I write these lines in Sydney, a beautiful pair of orange-breasted green parrots sit on the roof of the neighbouring building feeding their chick. If birds can feel like this and never abandon their babies, then how is it possible for human parents to give up their own children? Again and again. I cannot and will not believe that outdated customs combined with government policy can really force human beings to renounce that most beautiful and basic of human feelings, the parental instinct. It should not be possible, but it is.

6

Red Mary of the Orphanage

'I've never known who I was. My name was chosen for me by the missionary orphanage. They first gave me a foreign name, Mary, but during the Cultural Revolution, when I was in my thirties, the Red Guards changed it to Red Mary.'

ON THE evidence I have been able to dig up, the first orphanages in China date from the beginning of the twentieth century and were set up following the arrival of Western missionaries in China for the third time (the first two periods of missionary activity in China were during the Tang dynasty, AD 618–907, and in the thirteenth century). They were known as 'Children's Houses' or 'Gospel Institutes'. The very first was established in 1896 by the Protestant Anglo-American mission at the Church of the Four Saints in the city of Chengdu, Sichuan province, in memory of the missionary nurse Fu-ji-li.* It was followed by other Protestant orphanages in Chongqing, elsewhere in Sichuan, and in Fujian and Zhejiang provinces. There were Catholic orphanages too, more than 150 of them by 1920.

I have heard that, far back in history, there were Chinese government-run orphanages but as I have been unable to find any hard evidence, this remains just a piece of 'folklore'. Before 1990, all the Chinese orphanages I saw with my own eyes or was told about were places society had forgotten; the country and its

---

* 'Jili Fu' or Jenny Ford, a Canadian who went to Chengdu with the Women's Missionary Society and died there in 1897.

government simply could not be bothered with them. They were viewed as a national embarrassment by many officials, while the common people saw them as human rubbish dumps. The reaction, when you asked about local orphanages, was surprise. Nobody would put it quite so bluntly but the subtext was 'What do you want to go digging around in them for?' or, 'Those girls are rootless orphans, forget about them!'

While the rest of China had been torn apart by war and rocked by social and cultural changes for nearly a century, orphanages were almost completely forgotten. It was only with the revival of a (government-sponsored) civic consciousness in the 1990s that the public realised how dramatically their numbers had increased.

Towards the end of the 1980s I had visited a few orphanages and they were, without exception, unbearably sad places. To put it bluntly, a so-called orphanage in those days consisted of one room of no more than a dozen square metres, which not only functioned as the children's dormitory, but doubled as the office and sleeping space for a couple of workers too. In the better ones, a cramped kitchen might be attached. There was no inside toilet, no yard, and they lacked the most basic childcare equipment. There was, of course, nowhere for the children to play. However, by the 1990s, as the reforms finally percolated down to these forgotten corners of Chinese society, orphanages began to receive charitable funding from the newly wealthy. (Up until that time, almost no one, from the government elite to ordinary folk in small towns and countryside, had food or money to spare for orphans who would probably end up starving to death anyway. For the poor, it was all they could do just to keep body and soul together. Charity was out of the question.)

Hitherto, milk products had always been in short supply all over China. This meant that orphanages had to find different ways to feed the children: in north China, they were fed on a wheat flour porridge, in the south, it was rice gruel. Often, the endless wailing of hungry babies drove orphanage workers to take them into the nearest town in search of some good-hearted mother who had just given birth, and who was willing to put them to the breast for a few sucks.

My impression was that before the 1990s the main item of

expenditure for these orphanages was clothing and bedding. The babies were lined up on a long trestle, or squeezed in twos and threes into the kind of basket used in the countryside for storing dry goods. In better orphanages, it was one baby per vegetable basket. Most newborns in those days were swaddled in what was called a 'candle bag': that is, their hands and legs were bound straight to their bodies with soft wrappings of cotton or silk. Their lower limbs were completely enclosed, and just the face was visible, with the back and sides of the head protected by a corner of the wrappings, which formed a peak behind. If you stood the swaddled infant upright, it resembled a candle with a flame at the top.

I do not know if the 'candle bag' swaddling was named after this shape, but I do know that it was a form of swaddling commonly adopted by many nationalities in China, especially at night-time and in winter. I have since seen similar practices in other parts of the world, and have received similar explanations as to why it is done: to ensure that the newborn 'grows up healthy and beautiful'. In China, 'growing up healthy and beautiful' includes 'sleeping the back of the head flat', because we consider a flattened back of the head beautiful, and an 'oafishly protruding forehead and a spoon-shaped back of the head' as something to be avoided.

However, the orphanages were extremely short-staffed and the workers did not have the time or money to ensure that their charges grew up healthy, let alone beautiful. In fact they usually had so little bedding that in winter several babies had to share one small quilt, and in summer they went naked and had no protection against mosquitoes and other biting insects. When I made attempts to find out more about these orphans, no one, from the central government to the lowest officials in charge of orphanages, could provide me with any written records. Documentary evidence is in general sadly lacking for twentieth-century China.*

Then, in the 1990s, especially after the liberalising of government

* See my previous book, *China Witness*, an oral history compiled from the memories of elderly Chinese men and women, for an explanation of the reasons why.

policy on adoption and the growing involvement of Western adopting families, Chinese orphanages emerged from obscurity and began to occupy a central position in Chinese international policy. In no time at all, running orphanages became part of the economic boom and their numbers shot up. In my view, however, the two things in China which should not have been expanded and developed were, firstly, prisons and, secondly, orphanages. They needed to be reformed and improved, not to be used as a way of developing the economy. An increased number of prisons and orphanages is not a success story for any country – in fact, it is nothing less than a national tragedy.

To be perfectly honest, I have never to this day entered a Chinese orphanage where I felt the children received the kind of just and fair treatment they deserved. As late as 2007, when The Mothers' Bridge of Love funded medical treatment for a number of children and I tried to go and see them after they had recovered, I personally experienced the unrelenting pressures that orphanages were subjected to. In this case, we were making a courtesy visit to the staff with whom we had been working, in an orphanage which we had supported for years, but still we were turned away. The reason was that I had come from abroad and they suspected that we were digging up dirt on life in China for the Western media. The authorities had already punished one institution severely after an American adopting family secretly videoed the local community outside the orphanage, and then posted the footage on the Web. For the local government, this was evidence that 'the orphanage had inadequate surveillance and monitoring procedures, and the villagers' poverty had been used as a way for capitalism to attack socialism'!

Although this incident had not happened in 'our' orphanage, those which had contacts with the outside world had received warnings and, as a result, charitable organisations had become politically sensitive and harder to get into than Fort Knox. I quite understood the terror of local petty officials and orphanage managers, faced with a system where the law was unsound and the ground rules shifted constantly. They had had almost no specialist training, so how were they to manage aid and funds from overseas donors, and maintain a 'correct international image'? In any event, their decisions were not based on natural logic, but on such life-and-death (to them) considerations as 'What will my superiors think?' and 'Might I lose my job over this?'

There were three main kinds of orphanage staff in 'Red China'; that is, before the 1990s: those who had grown up in the orphanages themselves; supporters of local Buddhist temples; and women on their own, especially widows. (There were very few male workers.) The majority came from backgrounds which they had no wish to remember, and led a hopeless existence taking in, bringing up and burying orphans. Their only interest was in seeing the children go through set stages: *turn at three* (the babies should be able to turn over at three months); *sit at six* (they should be able to sit up at six months); *crawl at eight* . . . and so on. Their main aim was to find each child a family; her long-term interests and position in life had nothing to do with them. I was put out of the door over and over again with the words: 'Don't go telling stories in your programmes about these girls who have no families and no mothers!'

I had always wanted to interview someone who had worked in a senior position in an orphanage and could verify those few scraps of information I had been able to gather over a dozen or so years, but I had had no luck. But perhaps the Good Lord heard my prayers because, in the spring of 2007, when I was back in China to check a few final facts for *China Witness*, my persistence was eventually rewarded. I was passing through Shanghai on my way back to the UK when I happened to meet a retired orphanage worker.

*

I met her in a small noodle restaurant on Huaihai Central Road. She was the only solitary diner – every table except hers was occupied by couples – and after the waiter had taken my order, he told me we would have to 'pair up' at her table. She looked like something out of old Shanghai, completely out of place in the big modern city. I guessed she was between sixty and seventy years old; her white hair was coiled in an old-fashioned bun, a style worn nowadays only by a few dancers and long considered outdated. I remember that she was wearing a bronze-coloured linen-satin-mix jacket buttoned in the old-fashioned way slant-wise across her front and black jacquard-weave trousers underneath. Her shoes struck me particularly: they were the kind of embroidered cotton shoes, with pretty coloured uppers and soft, comfortable rubber soles which I had always loved. At that time, these varied in price considerably depending on the quality of the uppers and soles, and cost anything from 10 to 300 yuan.* In front of her on the table was a bowl of Yangchun (Shiny-Spring) noodles and two Shanghai-style side dishes: yellow fish and hairy beans marinaded in wine, honey and salt (which we call 'drunken' dishes). As I joined her, she was sucking in her noodles one at a time – yes, really! One at a time. I had only ever seen my son, Panpan, play 'kiddie games' with his food in this way, but never a grown-up.

When the old lady caught me watching her, she looked faintly embarrassed, and quickly put the noodle strand she was holding with her chopsticks back into her bowl, with a muttered: 'It's so long since I've had these noodles.' Her accent sounded southern Chinese, but I could not tell exactly where she was from. I felt embarrassed in my turn, and said, 'I'm sorry, I didn't mean to disturb you. I was just thinking I would order some of what you're having. It's a long time since I've had "drunken" vegetables too.'

'You don't live in Shanghai then?' She glanced at the other diners as if comparing me with them. My clothes must have looked very obviously what the Shanghainese would call 'provincial', in comparison to the designer outfits in which they were dressed.

'My family was originally from Shanghai, but I grew up in Beijing and other places. What about you?' I asked, my reporter's instincts coming to the fore.

'I'm originally from Shanghai too, but I left when I was quite young and I haven't been back since, until last month I got the opportunity, and I just can't believe my eyes, I really can't!' She pointed out of the window and at the restaurant's Western-style panel lighting.

---

* About $1.30/£0.70 to $39/£21 at the time (2007).

'And how long have you been away?' I put the question tentatively.

'Nearly sixty years . . .' She picked up a long noodle with her chopsticks, considering it thoughtfully.

'Sixty years!' I sensed reproving looks from the diners around us at my uncouth yelp.

'Yes, I left Shanghai in 1948,' she said, feeding each strand of noodle into her mouth with the utmost care.

My noodles soon arrived and I picked up a noodle and fed it slowly, section by section, into my mouth with my chopsticks. She smiled. 'You eat noodles that way too?'

'Uh-uh. You know the Chinese saying that if you eat in big mouthfuls, you're soon full, but if you eat in small mouthfuls, you savour the taste. I can see you're more of a connoisseur of food than I am, so I'm following your example.'

'Well, I don't know about that. I lived in an orphanage for many years. Big mouthfuls of the food we had then wasn't very good, and it was only a long time afterwards that you could eat small mouthfuls and feel full.'

I hoped she wouldn't notice my eyes light up at her answer, when I realised she could tell me so much. She did notice, though, and was surprised by my interest. I started simply by asking her what she did in the orphanage.

'I don't know that I should tell you. It's not something that's ever talked about, it's all past and gone now.' And she turned to look out of the window at the gaudy crowds of men and women hurrying by.

'Would you mind waiting just a minute? I'll be right back.' I went to the cash till and found the manager on duty. I told her I was willing to pay ten times my bill if I could reserve the table I was at, and would she please bring us a selection of typical Shanghai side dishes: cold chicken in rice wine, duck gizzards in wine, braised bean curd, and a selection of vegetables – bean sprouts, soy beans in soy sauce, all the kind of things my grandmother used to serve at home.

I went back to the table and told the old lady everything: I was writing a book. I had also set up a charity called The Mothers' Bridge of Love. I had never been able to find out anything about life in Chinese orphanages in the past . . . Finally, I begged her to tell me the story of her life in an orphanage.

She looked embarrassed. 'I don't think I should. It might upset people.' I knew what 'people' she was talking about.

'But you're retired now, aren't you? You've come back to Shanghai. Shouldn't you tell children what happened in the past? Otherwise, all the good work which all of you did will simply be forgotten, won't it?'

But she still hesitated. Then I told her some of the questions I had been asked in letters from Chinese girls adopted overseas, and how in almost every letter the same question came up: 'Why didn't my Chinese mummy want me?'

Her eyes misted over at this. 'If only they knew . . . their poor, poor mothers!'

'They don't know because no one has told them. That's what I'm trying to do, tell them what their mothers were thinking.'

'I don't know what their mothers were thinking, but I do know what they suffered.'

The extra snacks I had ordered arrived, and filled up our small table. The familiar food seemed somehow to spirit her back to her childhood. She looked at the food, then at me, then at the food again and then back at me: 'These are all the things I love best. All the time I was away, I dreamed about them!'

'Let's enjoy them together, and take our time about it. Then when we've finished eating, you can decide whether you want to tell me your story or not.' And I picked up a piece of duck gizzard and placed it in her bowl.

You could tell from the way we picked up each morsel and ate it that neither of us had had these traditional dishes for a very long time. It was almost as if we were afraid they might vanish for ever once we had finished our meal. We ate every scrap, down to the last morsel of food and the last drop of sauce, and when the waitress came to take the dishes away, I could see my companion's eyes following the plates as they were carried down to the end of the restaurant and disappeared from view through a door. Then her gaze shifted back to the table, which still held two cups of chrysanthemum tea and a dish of melon seeds – it is bad manners for the host to leave the table bare at the end of a meal, and a cup of tea and some melon seeds or peanuts are a symbol of hospitality.

She looked at her watch, and around her at the slowly emptying restaurant. It was now after half past one. Most Chinese eat lunch before one o'clock, and dinner at six o'clock in the evening; even those of us who have lived overseas or work in foreign companies in China, speak a foreign language and dress from top to toe in clothes with foreign labels, still have a Chinese stomach which no amount of money or new fashions anywhere can change.

Finally she sighed and said, 'Well, I haven't much time left to me, and even if it's against the rules, this is the last chance I have to do something good for those little girls!' And that was how I came to hear her story.

*

'I've never known who I was. My name was chosen for me by the missionary orphanage. They first gave me a foreign name, Mary, but during the Cultural Revolution, when I was in my thirties, the Red Guards changed it to Red Mary, though in the orphanage I was still called Mary. I'm an orphan. The missionary women said I was from a wealthy family, because when I was left in the orphanage window at about two weeks old, in 1931, the clothes I was dressed in were made of silk, with small pink flowers hand-embroidered on them. I was wrapped in a brocade shawl with baby birds embroidered in gold on a silver background, and apparently there was also a little hand-made bag, but I don't know what was in it. The missionaries all said something different – a silver bracelet, a silver locket, some Yuan Shikai dollars.* Anyway, it was put away for me, and I was told I'd get it when I was baptised, but later on it was all lost when one of the missionaries joined members of the Wang Jingwei puppet government fleeing south from Shanghai to Hong Kong in 1945.

'Everyone was in a state of panic. We had had special protection

---

* Yuan Shikai (1859–1916) was a Chinese general and politician who helped overthrow the last Qing Emperor of China, became the second President of the Republic of China, and finally attempted to revive the Chinese monarchy, with himself as emperor. (*Trans.*)

and support from the puppet government, so people in Shanghai said that we orphans were traitors who had sold out to the Japanese. I don't suppose you know this, but after 1945, traitors were all executed, and I think the only reason we weren't executed was probably that we had some protection from foreigners.

'Anyway, I'll start at the beginning: I grew up in the orphanage, and I remember we had to say our prayers every day before meals and before bed. I learned to read and write when I was very young, in Chinese of course, but we could all say a few sentences in English too: *Amen*, and *God bless you*, we said those every day. I started helping with the younger children when I was very young. Then, when I was seventeen, I became a proper "missionary" in the orphanage myself, although by then we weren't real missionaries. The Communist Party didn't believe in God. We'd heard they were going to ban religion, because it was the opium of the people, and they were going to insist that women should become communal property, too. The rumours flying around in those days were really frightening. We none of us had any contact with the outside world, except for one missionary who was the manager, and she never told us anything. We'd been brought up to do as we were told and not ask questions.

'One very cold night in 1948, she called us all together and told us to get ready to go south, and we'd be off when she gave the word. Before dawn the next morning we got on a boat. It was a small one, I don't think there was anyone else on it apart from us. Soon after we set out, we hit a big storm and we had to take shelter in Taizhou in Zhejiang province. When we were on shore, the orphanage manager ordered us not to speak to anyone else, and if we had to, we weren't to say which orphanage we came from. That was where I was formally baptised, but we didn't stay there more than a month. A big boat picked us up, and we were taken south to Fujian to wait for another boat to Hong Kong, but no more boats came after that and we stayed put.

'Soon after that, China was liberated and the local government looked after us the way the Wang Jingwei government had done. They provided food, and housed us in a church. We were Roman

Catholics, but this was an Eastern Orthodox church. When I think back on it now, I believe those worker and peasant cadres probably had no idea even what a crucifix was. Anyway, in those days, we were always hearing that the Guomindang nationalist government was going to launch a counter-attack on the mainland; and when we went out shopping we often saw anti-American and anti-British slogans which the Communist Party put up. And sometimes someone would slip a Guomindang propaganda tract or a speech by Chiang Kai-shek in with our purchases. I still don't know why they were all fighting each other.

'It wasn't long before there were more upheavals. Anyone who had helped the Japanese in the 1930s, or the Guomindang in the 1940s, or anyone who was anti-Communist in the 1950s, was a traitor to be rooted out. Our orphanage bore the brunt of it. The head missionary was put in prison, where she died soon afterwards. Our "imperialist-feudal orphanage" was disbanded. I remember that there were a dozen workers, and fourteen children between the ages of two and twelve. Anyone with family to go to was given a bit of money and sent to relatives. There were three of us workers, including me, who had nowhere to go. The boy babies were taken away – I think they were adopted but there were no proper procedures and no documentation in those days. I think the government was only just starting to make personal records of its citizens.

'So, the three of us workers who were left and eight little girls formed an "orphan group" and we were moved into a ramshackle old craft workshop, which had just a few rooms. They sent us a Party Secretary and we officially became a Patriotic Orphanage. In fact, we still did the same work as we'd done before, it was just that everything that had a religious connotation was abolished in our daily lives. I carried on quietly praying to myself, though. I was a girl who was married to God!

'As for the children . . . Some of them got married, and some of them became teachers – there was a shortage of people who could read and write, you see. In the end, only two were left. At first, we all had enough to eat, clothes to wear and a place to live, but after 1957, in the Three Years of Famine, that all changed. Especially after 1959, we heard of people dying of hunger. We hadn't taken in any babies for ten years, but now gradually people started to leave their children with us again, and that went on until the Cultural Revolution started in 1966. When we opened the orphanage door in the morning, we sometimes found a child already starved to death. Some had been dead for several days, and their parents still left them with us. Why? I wonder. Especially at the beginning of 1960, you saw people who'd starved to death every day. It wasn't so bad in winter, but when the summer came, the stench of rotting bodies was appalling. We were very lucky: we had guaranteed basic food rations. The cadre in the Food Distribution Department looked after us really well. Later we heard that he'd died of starvation himself. We cried when we heard the news. No one nowadays would believe that someone in charge of food supplies could die of hunger!

'When the Cultural Revolution began, I was dragged off to face "struggle sessions" and confess my "crimes". My four crimes were these: I was from a bad background (even though I didn't even know who my parents were – I knew nothing – but those little things which had been left with me when I was abandoned were the "evidence"). Secondly, I had sold out to the Japanese, and been their propaganda tool. (In fact, at the time when I was supposed to have been an emissary of the puppet government, I was only six or seven years old. How could I even know what traitor meant? It was ridiculous!) Thirdly, I had been a servant of US imperialist religion. (But I was a Christian, that was my faith, wasn't it?) Fourthly, I was a defector because I had tried to run away from the People's Liberation Army by going south. Ai-ya-ya! You didn't know whether to laugh or cry with those Red Guards. They thought that by calling me Red Mary they'd make me a revolutionary! Then they packed me off to a Reform through Labour farm in Hubei province. As soon as they found out there that I'd worked in an orphanage, they sent me to do my "reform through labour" in an orphanage in a small town near the city of Jingzhou.

'That was a miserable place, absolutely on its last legs. There were six babies under one year old laid out in a row on a mat on the floor for the bugs to bite. What kind of an orphanage was that? There was one old woman in her sixties, and she took care of the kids, and grew the food for herself at the same time. The children were just left to cry all day. She mostly fed them on rice gruel, and kept them clean by sluicing the urine and excrement off the mat with cold water. By night she slept squeezed on to the mat with the babies, at the mercy of the mosquitoes just as they were. When I think back on it, it was enough to make you weep! I couldn't live like that. It wasn't an orphanage so much as a place for killing babies.

'The next day, I went to see the cadre who'd sent me there, in tears, and told him what a miserable state the children were in. He was a middle-aged peasant, and when he heard my story he patted the bamboo slatted bed they used when it was hot in summer, and said: "This afternoon, I'll get two slatted beds sent over for you – one for the babies and one for you and her, and they can fix up mosquito nets too. I can't manage any more beds at the moment, so you and she will have to share. And in a couple of days, I'll send over a couple of 'educated youth',* to help with the gardening in the day time." And that's what happened. The old woman said it was the first time she'd ever slept in a bed! Then, when the girl students arrived, things got much better. They were so fond of the babies, and those six poor little mites finally began to put on some weight. They got so plump and rosy, everyone thought they were really sweet! Apparently, the parents of five of the babies had been killed during fighting in the Cultural Revolution, and one had been brought in by a Red Guard, who found her in the fields.

'The concept of orphanages didn't really exist outside of cities, back then. Killing girl babies was still taken for granted in the countryside, and even in city orphanages most of the babies simply died from neglect. Properly equipped orphanages weren't set up till later. Not in the mid-1980s, except maybe in big cities. Towns, and even smaller cities, didn't have real orphanages. They were called orphanages, but actually they were just one room, with a board bed and a couple of pots and pans for cooking. Just a place where a few poor little mites were looked after.

---

* Middle-school students sent to work in the countryside during the Cultural Revolution. (*Trans.*)

'Later I was transferred to other places in Hubei and Shanxi to set up orphanages, and I found there were no records to speak of. Hard to say why not. We Chinese don't document things like Westerners do – they have people keeping records up to date right from when an organisation is set up, including stuff to do with buildings and maintenance. But in China, everything gets burnt because people are afraid that the next lot of people in charge will punish them for any shortcomings they find out. It's a real pity!

'As far as I know, small country towns began to get proper orphanages like city ones only at the end of the '80s and beginning of the '90s. Peasants leaving the villages in search of work were one reason. If families couldn't bring themselves to kill unwanted babies, then the workers brought them to the towns, in the hope that they'd be taken in and looked after. Then there were the families who only wanted a boy baby, not a girl, and couldn't have another because of the one-child-per-family policy. They knew where to go to have the baby and where to go to abandon it. Then there were the city girls or students who got pregnant before marriage, I saw that myself, and there were plenty of those. They would leave a memento with their baby: a letter or a book, or some token of those times. That wasn't something the peasants would do. There was another reason why orphanages developed, and that was the liberalisation which made international adoption possible. It was foreign adopting families and the money they paid to the orphanages that made it possible to improve them.

'I don't even know how much it cost foreigners to adopt a baby. Strange that we worked in the business and we never knew. I do know that it costs anything up to 10,000 yuan for a Chinese family to adopt a baby boy.* The money must have gone into big officials' pockets – we never saw that kind of money in the orphanages. But the orphanages now are much better than they used to be. There's a world of difference in the food, the clothes

---

* She was shocked when I told her that foreigners could pay $3,000–$5,000 (c.£1,600–£2,600 in 2007) or anywhere from 25,000–45,000 yuan at the time to adopt a baby girl. And in fact it could cost a Chinese family as much as 10,000–50,000 yuan ($1,300–$6,500) to adopt a boy, but only 200–300 yuan ($25–$39) for a girl.

and the equipment that they have! I've seen orphanages that have turned into business enterprises. Still, even that's better than lining up the babies on the floor to be bitten to death by bugs.

'You don't know how hopeless the cadres in charge of the orphanages were, everywhere. They either just provided basic childcare and no education, because they couldn't read and write themselves, or they turned the orphanages into businesses, or used them as a springboard for their own career. When the foreigners came to adopt our babies, they treated them like rich VIPs. We had to dress the babies who were being adopted in nice new clothes, preferably things with foreign writing on, so as to keep up appearances. But those cadres didn't understand that the reason why foreigners despised us was precisely because we'd started flocking to junk food and Western fast food outlets like McDonald's! They were useless. They didn't even know the difference between Pinyin* and English! That's the kind of leaders we had! Our babies were wasted on people like them.

'It was only in about the year 2000 when migrant workers coming to the big city saw all those foreigners adopting Chinese baby girls that they realised that places which took in baby girls even existed. As for country cadres who had never left their home town in their lives, when they came to the cities to see how things were being done now, it put their heads in a spin. They went back home ordering orphanages to be set up right, left and centre. They saw them as a way to "solve the surplus population problem, bring in foreign money and develop the local economy", as they put it. And I know all this because since 1996 I've been invited all over China to advise on setting up orphanages. Otherwise, I would never have had the chance to come back to Shanghai.

'I'm an adviser to a number of orphanages now, it's what they call the "civil administration strategy". China really has no proper system for managing people and resources in civil administration, and people who've actually worked in orphanages like me are quite rare. I don't know what they mean by modernisation, let alone modernisation of orphanages, but I do know what I saw and experienced when I was growing up in an orphanage or

---

* Chinese written in letters of the alphabet, not characters, e.g. *Beijing*.

working in one. Besides, this is a way in which I can do some good for those poor little mites!

'And there are still a lot of abandoned babies. Every year after the harvest and after the Chinese New Year, migrants coming back to the city bring girl babies with them. There are a few boys, but very few, and they're usually the ones with some health problem. Sometimes city families will pick out a baby to send to an orphanage too, and hospitals always send abandoned babies there. And these are all girls. The parents simply disappear without a word.

'People even come to sell babies. I'm not sure I should tell you this, but I've already said such a lot so I might as well tell you everything. Children are bought and sold, and some orphanages do buy in children. Didn't I say that some cadres have turned it into a business, and business means buying and selling? Actually, that's where the funds for developing modern orphanages come from. The state is supposed to keep an eye on things. But what's the state if not people – the cadres who work in national administration? In any case, never mind the state, it's what happens at the grass roots that counts. China is too big, there are too many people, and changes have come too fast. I don't think anyone can keep tabs on everything that's going on, and certainly not what piddling little officials in orphanages are doing!

'So why did international adoption seem to slow down after 2006? It started when orphanages were set up in the north-west of China, maybe as part of economic development, and perhaps they wanted to shift the focus of international adoption to the north-west. The orphanages in the eastern cities are basically all empty now – there are only a few handicapped kids left that no one wants. But orphans in the central and western part of China aren't being properly looked after. I've seen places in Ningxia province where conditions are as miserable as they used to be in Hubei – there are no bugs in summer, but the winters are bitterly cold, and that's worse. Those poor babies! You can't imagine.

'And the children's mothers . . .? Some just leave their children and slip away; others come back and ask me how they're doing. At the beginning, they'll say they are asking on someone else's behalf, but once the baby is registered at the adoption centre, and sometimes after they've been taken away by the adoptive parents, a mother will come and let me know in a roundabout sort of way that she's the birth mother. Oh, those poor women must miss their daughters so much. They don't care if people sneer at them, and they're prepared to risk being fined by the Family Planning Office for having more than one child, but still they come and ask about their babies. But there's a bit of the Guan Yin in orphanage workers, and they're kind enough to keep quiet about it. Those poor women, some of them miss their babies so much it drives them mad. Ay! I can't begin to tell you!

'I often think that if my own mother had found any other way, she definitely wouldn't have left me in an orphanage! When I was young, I spent every day working with the children, but I didn't have any particular feelings about it. Then when times got tough there was no time for thinking, it was hard just to get enough to eat and sleep. It was only when life settled down that I thought how every little bundle that came with a baby was filled with the mother's love! Mothers used to leave little keepsakes with their babies. But I don't think any of the places where I worked kept these. Like everything else, they were thrown away. I've written to the authorities about this many a time, but they take no notice. It's not that the mementoes are valuable, but they're evidence about the child's life. But the orphanage administrators just told me that there was no space to keep "rubbish" like this. Sometimes it went straight into the stove as kindling, that very day!

'There were all sorts of little tokens! Even words. A few mothers had written long, heart-breaking letters on the baby's clothing. Others had embroidered things, or sewn some little crosses or Xs on the cloth. The poorest would make a fingerprint in blood! Some babies looked as if they'd come with nothing – until you looked closely at a little fingernail and saw there was a cross or an X on it. Perhaps the parents were too unhappy and their circumstances too difficult to do anything else – but didn't they realise the baby's fingernails would grow and be cut? We never photographed them, we never thought of that back then, and how many orphanage workers could afford cameras in those days?

'They rarely had distinguishing marks on their skin. But plenty of babies came with scars, mostly between their legs. I asked some midwives about that, and they all said the same thing: it was burns from an oil lamp or candle wax. The first thing the village midwives did when the baby was born was not to clear its airway but to check whether it was a boy or a girl, because that was what the whole family was waiting to hear. Some of the burns were on the baby's private parts, and the moisture there made it difficult for the poor little things to heal.

'It's true that the babies are too young to know what's going on, but their mothers suffer so much loving them. It's a bit better for educated women – at least they know that their babies are being adopted overseas, mostly by well-off families, and will be treated as daughters, not as child brides or as slave labour. I feel sorry, so very sorry, for the uneducated ones. They've had such hard lives themselves, and then on top of the pain of giving birth to a daughter, they spend their time imagining all the awful things that the foreign families are doing to their little daughters. Do you know, they sometimes beg me to pass messages to the foreigners: don't make the child start work too young or she may not grow properly. Don't add too much water to the milk or rice porridge, or she might get hungry. Some say: she's got such a lot of black hair and if she likes it, plait it up for a few days. Don't cut her plaits off to save on hair-washing. Some of them want the new parents to "cradle her in your left arm, so the sound of your heartbeat will make her sleep better"!

'Those poor women, carrying their babies in their bellies for nine months, giving them up is like having their own flesh sliced out. They can't cuddle their own daughters, and they have no idea how the new parents are treating them. They spend their whole lives anxiously fearing for their daughters . . .'

Mary's voice trailed off – it was too painful for her to go on – and I too was sunk in thought. How those women suffered from having to part with their children. I forgot to turn off the tape recorder, and it was only when I transcribed the conversation later that I realised what a long time we had sat there in silence at that small restaurant table.

At the end of our talk, Mary gave me two names, Na and another Mary, whom I've called Green Mary. Na, she said, often travelled between Shanghai and the USA, while Green Mary was a top-level official in Beijing. Both, she said, could tell me more about how and why infants were abandoned. She also asked me to change her name when I wrote up what she had said, to mail her the original recording and, finally, not to contact her again. I told her that many of the women I interviewed made the same request, and promised to respect her wishes. But I knew that her story, and those of the mothers in her story, would never leave me . . .

As we said goodbye, Mary said to me: Print what I said, please, so those little girls can read it and will never forget their Chinese mothers.

As I was writing the first draft of this chapter, on 13 February 2008, a solemn ceremony of apology was being held in Australia. On behalf of the Australian government, Prime Minister Kevin Rudd apologised to the indigenous Australian children removed from their mothers to 'be educated'. And in Darling Harbour, Sydney, there is a 100-metre-long 'welcome wall' with the names of countless immigrants listed on it. I felt then that civilisation and democracy had finally prepared the way for many races to co-exist in Australia. That country of immigrants has finally been honest about its past and is now trying to provide a compassionate space where children may in future grow up peaceful and healthy in their own mothers' arms.

7

The Mother Who Still Waits in the USA

'I can't write this story myself and it's been weighing on me for all these years.'

I HAVE MET very few Chinese mothers who know anything about how daughters are brought up in Western families. Most of these mothers live a lonely existence, unable to share their burden with anyone. And any hope on the part of adopting families that their Chinese children may one day have the opportunity to thank their birth mothers for keeping them alive can only be remote. Finding the child's birth mother is like looking for a needle in the proverbial haystack, given how far the West is from the sources of information, and how scant those sources are in China. Before the 1990s most ordinary Chinese in the countryside had no right to a birth certificate or similar personal legal record. In addition, the secrecy with which the Chinese government guards adoption information is compounded by the different ways things are done locally and by the sense of shame which has traditionally surrounded adoption. In mainstream Chinese culture, when people abandon or give up their children for adoption, or get divorced, outsiders do not get involved. These are considered as much private matters between husband and wife as their sex lives. Many families do not even tell children they have been adopted. A child-less family is a tragedy; a couple without children have failed.

Babies have been abandoned in China since time immemorial. Ordinary folk did it because they believed that they owed it to the ancestors to give them a son and heir as the first-born. The gentry and imperial families did it, frequently, in order to protect wealth and interests. At no level of society did anyone want to admit that the flame at the ancestral shrine which could only be kept alive by the eldest son might go out. This extended to the very top of society: every emperor had to be 'the real thing', their powers and privileges rightfully inherited.

Divorce as we understand it today in China is a product of modern Chinese society. Up until the overthrow of the feudal imperial system in 1911, a man could get rid of his wife, but a woman had absolutely no rights to end her marriage. Then with the violent upheavals and political turmoil of the twentieth century, divorce (and remarriage) came to be regarded as a way up the political ladder and to a better life. No one would frankly admit to anyone else that the reason for their divorce was to escape from a marriage so loveless it was unnatural. It was not until the 1980s that Chinese people were able to decide freely about marriage, to make up their minds and look for the kind of family that they really wanted. From that point on, 'divorce' finally became a topic which people talked about openly.

Adoption, in old China, meant taking on the child of a relative. It applied mainly to boys, who joined the adopting family and then shared in the distribution of its wealth. Girls were hardly ever adopted in this way. They normally went to a new family as child brides, reared till they were old enough to be married off to the son of the family. Before this system was abolished in 1950, almost all child brides suffered a cruel fate: they did not enjoy equality with the other daughters or have the normal rights that came with marriage into a new family, and were used as cheap labour from an early age. Traditional feelings about blood relationships remained immensely strong, linked as they were to property inheritance and the duties of children to care for elderly parents. People were afraid the adopted children, whom they had brought up with such sacrifice, might leave their adopted family once they were grown-up and go back and care for their birth parents – who, after all, had taken no part in their upbringing. So adopted children were rarely told the facts about their origins.

These attitudes began to change from 2005, as the government encouraged Chinese families to adopt abandoned children. However, in practice, very few are able to: deeply rooted social attitudes and the one-child policy militate against it. Even if they do, how will the rest of society react? And will adopting families or those giving up their children succeed in overcoming traditional prejudices and creating a new concept of the family? All these questions need to be explored, and I think it may take some time.

When I set up the charity The Mothers' Bridge of Love, its aims were to help adopting families learn more about the birth mothers' lives and Chinese history and culture, and to form a bridge between the receiving society and the children's birth culture. Finding out more about the mothers who had been forced to give up their babies was the most difficult part of the process. I had come across such mothers in my work as a journalist in China, but to find out any more, I needed to have the right contacts at all levels of government. The combined weight of tradition and administrative inertia had made that impossible at the time, so it was a task which I was still working on.

I knew that I had to take every opportunity to uncover the stories of these mothers, so I did my best to see the women to whom Mary had given me an introduction: Na and Green Mary. Red Mary had said they would be able to tell me more about how and why infants were abandoned. But I was unable to contact Na in China. I did not meet her until October 2007, when I was doing a tour for my Mothers' Bridge of Love book, in the USA. A friend of hers had been at a meeting I held in Boston with some adopting families. The next day, many emails from new friends dropped into my in-box, but there was only one in Chinese: the woman introduced herself as Mary's contact, Na. She was now an American citizen, and wrote that she hoped we could meet if I had time in New York.

I had already planned to spend some time in New York buying Christmas presents so I leapt at this chance to meet Na. We arranged to meet in a coffee shop on Broadway. To my surprise, when I arrived it was thronged with bustling crowds, even before ten o'clock on a weekend morning. I waited for a free table near the window and managed, with some difficulty, to get one. I was still ten minutes early, but Na seemed to have stuck to good Chinese habits, and turned up early too. I spotted her as soon as she came through the door, probably because it was unusual for a Chinese woman to come into a coffee shop on her own. And she, after a cursory glance around, came unhesitatingly in my direction.

Na looked no more than thirty years old. I saw she was dressed, not in casual European style, nor in designer labels and expensive jewellery like a Chinese woman, but with the sort of expensive chic of the typical New Yorker. She wore a pale pink and blue checked jacket, with a round collar and large buttons, under which was visible a cream, high-necked cashmere top. Her jewellery consisted of a glittering braided gold necklace and matching earrings. She wore cream trousers with turn-ups and a pair of white leather ankle boots with ornamental gold buttons which matched her jewellery.

Na took off her coat and sat down, the picture of cream-coloured elegance. She started by questioning me about the things that The Mothers' Bridge of Love was doing, and we went on to discuss the difficulties facing charities run by Chinese people overseas, and the lack of recognition and support for them in the West. Gradually, the conversation turned from how to help Western families understand Chinese culture, to the letters we received from adopting families asking for help. Several times Na's eyes filled with tears and she seemed agitated. Finally, her emotions overcame her and she said in a trembling voice:

'I know my daughter's among them!'

I was mystified. 'Your daughter?'

'Yes, my daughter. She was only with me for thirty-two days! Then I abandoned my own child!' And she burst into tears.

I gasped in horror. How could this chic young woman, obviously doing so well for herself in the USA, have abandoned her own daughter? However, I took hold of myself. This was not the time to leap in with questions. I hoped a quiet interval while we drank our coffee would calm us both down. A waiter came to the table and asked if we were all right.

I watched while Na carefully dabbed at the tears on her impeccably made-up face with Chinese 'Heart to Heart' paper handkerchiefs. Then she clasped her coffee cup in both hands, as if to stop them trembling, and looked out of the window to the avenue which stretched away down to Central Park.

'In 2002, in my final year at Shanghai University, I had an affair with my professor. Back then, I was a lively, irresistible young woman, or so I thought. My parents were both teachers in another university. They brought me up very strictly and never allowed me to go out by myself. It was not until my fourth year at university, when I was twenty-two, that they let me move into the college dormitory. Shanghai at the end of the '90s had been transformed by the economic reforms. It had become "Westernised", and young women certainly had a great deal of freedom. Even in their first year, many girl students used to sleep with their boyfriends, and there was a lot of rivalry over men. I was the ugly duckling in my eight-girl dorm. Everyone laughed at me for being such an old-fashioned virgin, a girl who wanted a boyfriend but didn't have one. It got me down so much that sometimes I felt I was worth less than a prostitute. At least they knew about being a woman, and how to give a man a good time. Luckily it was early autumn when I moved in, and I still had a mosquito net round the bed to hide my gloom. ('Student blues' we used to call it then.)

'Anyway, when it got dark at night, those nets seemed like a protective shield for the other girls, and they would open up about their love lives. They talked about everything, no holds barred, from their boyfriends' looks to their dicks, from how to make love to what it was like having an orgasm. To be honest, looking back on it, I can hardly believe it happened. The generation of students that came before us, even when they became parents, never even held hands in front of their children, or embraced or kissed. How come we jumped suddenly to the other extreme? I never had any practice at going out on my own, like my classmates did. I'd gone from being cloistered at home straight to being surrounded by all this steamy sex talk. It was really a struggle for me to cope.

'Sometimes I'd find myself breathing hoarsely and it would throb down there!' She paused and looked keenly at me: 'I expect you're shocked at me speaking so frankly! We Chinese are two-faced, you know. We were brought up to be. Even biological instincts are seen as black and white, and divided into the good ones and bad ones. The truth is that we all repress a lot of memories in the process of growing up. It's not that we don't want to open up to other people, it's because we can't admit them to ourselves. But then these memories become scourges which lash us in our dreams! I'm sorry, I'm beginning to sound quite wicked.'

This was when I brought out my tape recorder, and asked if I could record her words.

'Just so long as you do it as you did in *Good Women of China* and don't use my real name. I'm in engineering, I'm from the computer-bashing generation. I can't write this story myself and it's been weighing on me for all these years. So if you want to use it, then go ahead!' And she held out her hands, palms up, as if offering me her heart as well as her permission. Then she continued her story.

'Listening to the other girls gradually seemed to break down some of the moral defences my parents had set up around me for twenty years. Don't look at me like that. I'm telling you the truth,' she insisted. 'At first my reactions were purely physical; emotionally I wasn't very interested. I wasn't in any hurry. However, things began to change one night in late autumn when the talk turned to the youngest professor in our department.'

'I wasn't interested in having elevated academic discussions with him, and I wasn't like the other girls who were envious of his lovely family – a pretty wife, who was a cashier in a foreign-owned hotel, and boy-and-girl twins at home. It was nothing like that. What really interested me was the fact that he showed absolutely no interest in any other women. He seemed completely immune to temptation. I was amazed at his faithfulness, and intrigued at what love could turn someone into. For two months, I followed him, watched where he went and what he did. His behaviour really was irreproachable. If he wasn't in college, in the baths or in the office, then he was at home.

'He lived on campus. They had a corner flat, just a couple of floors up, and especially at night, it was easy to get a view inside from different angles. There was just a playing field outside their flat, no other buildings, so they hardly ever pulled the curtains. It seemed like he was good around the house, at least I often saw him doing the cooking, and when it came to the weekend you would see them holding their babies and chatting to the grandparents. It was enough to make anyone envious!

'I was convinced that he'd never noticed me spying on him, but one day he called me into his office. Nothing too unusual in that – we were in his class that term, after all – but as soon as I went in, he came straight to the point: 'Why are you following me?' I wanted to vanish through a crack in the floorboards. I must have gone scarlet!' And Na cupped her face in her hands with a smile.

'I decided simply to tell him the truth. I told him I wanted to find out if happy families really did exist, and if there was such a thing as a faithful man nowadays. He asked me: 'And is there? Have you found the evidence?' I said, 'I think so – it's you!' He looked taken aback. After a pause he said, 'You know, men aren't the same as women. They react differently not just psychologically but physiologically. They're different in their feelings, the way they look at things, their feelings about sex and responsibility.'

'I was disappointed by his po-faced answer. Any book about relationships between men and women would have told me exactly the same thing. I had expected something more profound from him.

'But then on another occasion he called me into his office, and this time what he said shocked me: "Don't be taken in by everything you see and hear. I'm not really the virtuous man you imagine. Not a day goes by without me having lustful thoughts. I've done my wife wrong too. We weren't married then but we were going out together, and I was seeing another woman at the same time. To be honest, it was having the twins that stopped me straying. They seemed to put a noose around my heart. And I couldn't bear to hurt the woman who had given me two such adorable babies! Na, stop dreaming about the perfect man. The reason why I've told you my secret is so that you and your aspirations for love won't be hurt. You're not the same as the other girls. They're experienced. Sexual experience for a woman is like the bark of an old tree. Every time a man and a woman have a good time together it leaves a scar on the woman which never heals! But the things men look for and worry about are the same things as women. They care about virginity too, and they're looking for the same answers as you are. So whatever you do, don't be led astray. That would hurt your boyfriend if he's a virgin."

'I never uttered a word that day, but my teacher's words kept going round and round in my head. When night came, I wrote them down and put lots of question marks and exclamation marks. I didn't know why I was doing this, but gradually as things happened, one by one, the question marks all turned into exclamation marks.

'One day, soon afterwards, I went to talk to him about my dissertation. I don't even know how it happened myself, but after a moment or two I looked him straight in the eye and found myself saying, "Will you touch me? The way a man touches a woman?"

'"Why?" he asked.

'I said, "I want to be awakened. I want to experience what it's like when a man and a woman are together."

'He looked at me for a long time, and then with one hand he half pulled, half pushed me behind the door of his office. I thought he was going to push me out, but just at the instant when I expected him to open the door, he began gently stroking the small of my back with one of his hands. Then he caressed my ears and my neck, and from there he put his hand inside my underclothes . . . that was the first time I'd been touched by a man, and all of a sudden my heart started pounding. I instinctively turned my mouth up towards his face, but he put his other hand over my mouth and said gently, "You should keep that for your man." Then he pulled out the hand that he had thrust inside my clothing, opened the door, and said "Goodbye."

'I don't have any idea how I got back to the dorm or what I had for dinner that night. You may laugh, but it was as if his hand was still on my skin. In my mind, I even moved it round to my chest and then downwards, and imagined the pleasure a man and woman give each other. I floated around for days feeling his hand on my body.

'That weekend, my parents, who were retired, were due to go on a three-week trip with some other pensioners to Guilin, and asked me to go home and look after the house. So I did. The flat was echoingly empty, and as I sat there alone I could still feel the professor's hand, as though it had got bigger and was doing just what it wanted to me. Finally, I couldn't stand it any more. I went to see him on the pretext that my father had some articles he had translated and wanted the professor to check some English words for him. The whole university knew how good his English was. He thought a bit and then said that the next weekend his wife was taking their children to see her parents in Hangzhou, so he could spare some time in the evenings to come and help.'

*

Listening to her, I was terrified by Na's boldness, even all those years later. I couldn't believe the professor would actually come to the house. But he did.

'He came in carrying a big dictionary,' Na went on, 'and asked where my father was. I told him he'd had to go out and would be back soon. Then I offered to make him a cup of tea. While it was brewing, I took off all my clothes and, completely naked, went up behind him holding the tea tray in my hands. He was browsing through the books on my father's bookshelf and without looking around pointed to a leaflet about a new imprint of the *Si Ku Quan Shu*,* and sighed: "Ai-ya! I've so wanted to buy those volumes but sadly, I can't afford them. Is your father thinking of collecting them?"

I didn't answer. I just put the tea down and stood behind him with my hands at my side!

'I felt very calm. Much better to give my body to this sincere man now than to who knows whom, at some point in the future, and besides, I felt I was honestly rewarding him. Since I hadn't said

---

* An enormous encyclopaedia compiled between 1773 and 1782 by edict of the Qing dynasty Emperor Qianlong. (*Trans.*)

anything, it was probably the sound of my breathing that made him turn around. He stood just inches from my naked body. For a few seconds he was shocked, but not for long. He flushed deeply and seized me in his arms, kissing and caressing me hungrily . . . and that was the beginning of our love affair in my house. We were in each other's arms every minute of every night that week!'

'And during that week, didn't it occur to you to ask whether he was a good man or a bad man?' I knew how many Chinese women felt guilty as they made love.

'He was just a man. Our generation is different from yours. We didn't trouble ourselves about guilt, or what was good and what was bad.'

'What about afterwards?' I couldn't help asking, as I imagined the scenes between the two families.

'There *was* no afterwards. At the end of the week, he went to collect his wife and children and went back to his family life. It wasn't awkward when we saw each other. As for me, well, I suppose everyone has an initiation, don't they? Anyway, that was what I thought. And my fellow students seemed all to have had the same kind of experience.

'He seemed to take it even more matter-of-factly than I did. *Come on, Xinran*' – (she said the words in English), seeing the expression on my face – 'It was lust, not love. I think that's the biggest difference between our generation and the previous one, and the ones before that. Right from the start, we treated sex, affection and love as separate parts of life, even someone like me with no experience. With my parents' generation, if you had the first two, then love had necessarily to follow, otherwise you were a slut. But in reality, you were living in a hypocritical, repressive culture!'

When I was listening to Na's tape I came across these words and they forced me to reflect. Had our generation really been so blighted in our love lives? Na told me that their one-week affair had had an unexpected outcome. The next time she had returned home from university, her mother noticed her daughter's thickened figure. Her parents were livid at this man who was neither husband nor fiancé and was offering their daughter nothing. As a couple they had always maintained a polite distance, but now they had a huge row. The father wanted to force Na to have an abortion; the mother disagreed. She said the baby had already been formed in the womb, and could not just be killed off. But they did agree on one thing: Na's disgrace had caused the whole family to lose face, right back through the generations. So they decided to spend all their money on sending their only child to study in the USA. She was to leave as soon as the Birth Month was up, and preferably settle there, get herself a job and a husband, and bring no further shame on the family.

*

'My daughter was an "autumn baby", born at full term and weighing four kilos,' Na told me. 'I had gone to a relative of my mother's who lived a long way away to have her. When she first put her little mouth to my nipple, I felt profoundly moved by this little creature's trust and dependence on me! I called her Xinxin, "heart to heart" – mine and hers. I had plenty of milk – lots of home-cooked Chinese dates and pig's trotters saw to that – and she grew into a plump little cherub. When the Birth Month was up, my parents booked two rooms for us in a hotel in Changzhou, a city where we didn't know anyone. My mother was worried I couldn't cope with the baby on my own, so we shared one room, and my father took the other.

'They wanted me to leave my daughter in an orphanage – and they spent three days and two nights working on me with a mixture of threats and persuasion. I held my baby in my arms, wept, knelt down and begged them not to make me give her up. They cried too, and begged me to do it. We all cried. Finally, my father had a recurrence of his heart trouble and had to be taken to hospital. My mother and I took it in turns to look after him and the baby. Every time I took my turn at the hospital with my father, I was frantic with anxiety that my mother would make a decision and do something without telling me. Soon my mother fell ill from exhaustion. We were strangers in Changzhou and I found it incredibly hard, looking after two old people and a month-old baby. But little Xinxin gave me the strength to go on.

'One day, my mother made me a sort of "deathbed" speech.

"All our lives," she said, "your father and I have fought to present a united front to everyone so that no one could say bad things about us when we were dead and gone. But if our only child lives as a single mother, how can your father and I go home to Shanghai? Never mind about passing our last years in peace and comfort, we simply couldn't face our friends and family. I didn't force you to have an abortion because I'm a mother, and I felt it wouldn't have been fair on a living creature to get rid of it like that, but we're just not brave enough to face the kind of life that you and your baby will bring us! You're twenty-two and our only child, and we've looked forward to you growing up ever since you were inside me. You've only been a mother for a month and you don't want to give up your daughter, but you haven't thought about how your old parents will cope with all the upset that this child is going to bring! I'm begging you, child, I'm begging you! You can see how ill it's made your father, and you must have seen how ill it's made me . . . I've found out that the children from all these orphanages around here are adopted by American families. If your daughter is adopted by them, who knows, one day you may be able to find her in America. Technology keeps on moving on, so there must be a way. We haven't got much longer to live, please give us a peaceful old age!"

'So that was how I finally made my decision to give up my child for adoption, because I thought I'd be able to find her again in America!' She shook her head slowly and looked down at the table. There was a silence, and suddenly I was aware again of the noise of the busy café all around us.

'And have you found her?' I asked at last.

'Not yet. It was not until 2005 that I discovered that there are 30,000 adopted Chinese children in the States.'

'Does your daughter have any distinguishing birthmarks?' I was thinking that I could post up a message on The Mothers' Bridge of Love website.

'No, she was a perfect little girl. Her right ear was a bit bent because I always held her in my left arm and it got squashed. But only a little, and it might have straightened out as she slept in a different position.

'I couldn't take her to the orphanage myself. My mother took her. She told them she'd found the baby in the street. I'll tell you what really, really hurts: I had wanted us both to have a keepsake, something to know each other by, so I got the top I used to wear when I was breast-feeding her and laid it edge to edge with the garment I was going to put her in, and with an indelible red pen I wrote three big characters, half on one, half on the other: Xinxin – two heart characters – and the character for "love". I hoped we'd always have this way of identifying each other, if at some time in the future we could match them up again. But when my mother came back from the orphanage, she said the children were all dressed in the same clothes. She was told that no children kept the things they were sent with, and if my mother didn't want them, then they'd just be incinerated. I spent that evening clutching my baby's remaining clothes. I didn't cry. It was a strange feeling, as if the terrible pain I felt had burned all my tears dry.

'My mother never told me which orphanage she'd taken her to, but before I left China for the first time, I went desperately looking for it. I finally found out which one it might have been, but I was told that it had been pulled down and the twenty-one children in it had been distributed to four other orphanages in nearby towns. Where had my daughter gone? Each time I come home, I follow up more leads. When I found Red Mary, she managed to get some information for me, but the government's scant adoption records are a closely guarded secret, and there's no way of verifying it. So far, the only thing I've been able to confirm is that my daughter was probably adopted by an American family.'

'Maybe one day DNA technology will become so common that it'll even be on our records. Then you could find your daughter easily. If that happened, would you ask for her back?'

'No, I couldn't do that.'

'Because you're concerned that your parents wouldn't accept her, or would feel they'd lost face?'

'I don't care about that. I told my present husband about her before we married. He's an American, and he loves children, so he understands. I couldn't ask them for my daughter back because I've seen with my own eyes how precious their Chinese children are to Western families. It's true she's my flesh and blood, and she'll be part of my life as long as I live. But adopting families bring up their children day by day, year after year, and they've become part of their lives too, part of the soul of the family. I couldn't break up their family and break their hearts . . . The pain I carry around with me is part of me, and I'm used to it. I'll bear it on my own!'

'So then, why do you want to find your daughter?'

'I want to put my arms around her. I want the little Xinxin I remember to turn into this grown-up daughter. I've missed her and worried about her so much, I want the comfort of seeing her with my own eyes and holding her in my arms. I want to see her grown-up and carefree. I'd even like to hear my Chinese daughter speak a bit of fluent English! And I'd like to give her the garment with my half of the three characters, so she would know how very, very much her Chinese mother loved her . . .'

The tears trickled down Na's face and dripped into her coffee cup. So did mine. The tears of two Chinese women mixed in with Western coffee.

*

When I was writing the first draft of this chapter, I discussed Na's story with my husband Toby Eady – who never knew his birth father, lost during the Second World War. I asked him when he had first missed his birth father. He told me it was when, in his early teens, he started to make his own decisions and wondered what the future held for him. That was the moment when he would have liked to turn to his birth father. The urge was extremely strong, and left him floundering emotionally between birth father and adopted father. But he could not reject his adopted father, because it was the love of his adopted family that had made him what he is today. I absolutely agreed with this way of putting it. He was right. We can none of us choose our birth parents, but your adoptive parents have adopted you body and soul. You have become part of two families, in every sense. But still I know that Na must look at the face of every six-to-seven-year-old Chinese girl she sees in New York, and wonder . . .

*

After I had returned to London I received an email from Na, saying that Red Mary, the woman who brought us together, had died suddenly of a heart attack at the end of November 2007. With her death, my plans to talk to her again and find out more of her story came to an end too. But in her way Mary had already bequeathed to me the stories of many, many Chinese women. Rest in peace, Mary, I will do my best to tell those Chinese girls about your life and how you loved them like a mother, even though you never knew your own.

8

A Morality Tale for Our Times

'What's nature? What's mother love? ... You've been to these villages? You've seen what pitiful lives village girls lead? They only survive at all by good luck!'

A T THE end of the 1980s, when I first started as a radio presenter, I found it hard to get anyone to tell me what they were *really* feeling in an interview. Some people were too afraid of being punished for what they said, others just didn't know what to say because no one had ever listened to them before. Some people would talk, but only in broad generalisations, and wouldn't talk about their own feelings, because they'd never been taught to understand them. I was at my wits' end, as I had grown up in the same society as my listeners. One day I was making red bell-pepper dumplings for my young son, Panpan, and a pepper seed stuck to my face. I didn't realise, so it stayed there. I took the bus to work that day, and another passenger, a woman, pointed at my face and said, 'You've got something red on your face.' I thanked her and wiped it off, and we sat chatting for a while. That woman was the first person who told me the story of her life.

That evening I thought long and hard about what had happened, and finally realised that I could use women's passion for detail as a way into their emotional world. So from that day on, I always made sure I put on my make-up a little bit care-lessly. Any small defect could be turned into a really useful tool:

a woman would come up to me and point it out, and I would say thank you and start chatting to her. I gradually learned how to use my own lack of knowledge to unlock the secrets of Chinese women. To remind myself what that bus passenger had taught me about women's awareness of each other and ability to communicate, I started painting just one fingernail. I called it my 'red spot'. And if I ever began to feel either superior or inferior, it also served as a reminder over the years to keep my feet on the ground.

But this technique has never really proved useful when dealing with government officials and other bureaucrats, where very different skills were required. In November 2006 there was a radical shift in China's adoption policy, as a result of which the rate of adoption slowed dramatically, single parents were turned down, and strict controls were imposed on the age of adopters. Overseas adopting families argued over the reasons. Was it because of the 2008 Beijing Olympics, or because the government was about to launch another political campaign, or because the one-child policy was to be abolished? Anxious adopters and would-be adopters all over the world flooded The Mothers' Bridge of Love with emails.

We decided to investigate why the adoption policy had changed, but we got nowhere: our emails, letters and phone calls all went unanswered, and all we had to go on was an announcement on the China Centre of Adoption Affairs (CCAA) web page, apologising for delays in processing applications. Government regulations laid down that the workings of China's adoption agency must never be revealed to foreigners – just like its secret service, in fact.

As someone born and brought up in China and steeped in its culture, I know that where the front door says 'No Entry', one has to try the back door. Many believe that this provides more reliable information in any case. However, now that China's reforms are well established, the government has begun to legitimise these back-door channels of information and put them to unconventional uses. For example, they leak misinformation so that people lose trust in leaks. Information leaked via the 'back door' is also used to resolve disputes at the 'front door', or to back up official sources, or to tighten controls over local government.

During 2006 and 2007, I tried different approaches and finally established contact with three officials working at different levels on adoption. They told me that the rumours I had heard were basically true. Firstly, the economic boom on China's eastern seaboard had brought a rise in living standards and so there were fewer orphans to adopt. Even the numbers of babies brought into town by migrant workers to be abandoned had fallen considerably. There was another reason, and it was connected with the new policy to open up north-west China, a huge, as yet under-developed area. It was hoped that economic development would enable local government to build a network of social welfare institutions in this poverty-stricken region. Foreigners were keen to help China's orphanages, and the funds they provided could help kick-start this process.

The sticking point, however, was how to staff the orphanages adequately. Life was hard in the north-west, standards of education were poor, and the wages and benefits offered to orphanage staff there were consistently lower than elsewhere in China. Being transferred to the north-west was like going back to the bad old days, and experienced staff from elsewhere in China, especially those with families, were prepared to resign or accept demotion rather than take a post there. The local staff, on the other hand, were ill-educated and had had almost no contact with foreigners. So the thing that was slowing up the pace of the transfer of adoption centres from the east to the west of China was the need to train staff capable of dealing with overseas adoption procedures.

There was also a third reason: there had been an increasing number of reports in local newspapers alleging mistreatment and sexual abuse of Chinese adopted children and the use of child labour by adopting families in the West. Chinese public opinion had turned against the West and people began to condemn the government's adoption policy. The result was a widespread climate of fear: orphanages put the brakes on their work with overseas agencies and some rejected overseas funding completely. They did not want to be punished for the offence of 'illicit relations with foreigners', or for any negative reports which might appear in the foreign media.

The concept of civil (that is, non-governmental) organisations is new in China, and one that baffles everyone from central government down to the ordinary people. There are several reasons for this general prejudice. Firstly, there have been many periods in Chinese history when they have in fact been illegal. Secondly, before 2005 even top government officials regarded charity work as a religious practice. After all, in their view, orphanages and other welfare institutions had all been set up by the Protestant Christian Church in the old days. And freedom of religion in China still exists in name only. Finally, ordinary people believed that doing charity work might make the rich richer and the famous look good, but they were sceptical that the poor got anything from doing good deeds.

It was only after 1980, with the economic reforms, increased social stability, and improvements in the standard of living, that attitudes began to change and it became accepted not only that charity made you feel good, but that families needed love and the country needed its families.

Most of those who worked in the CCAA had previous experience of working with foreigners in some capacity. You could get out of them information of a sort, written on the government's red-letterheaded paper. But it was not part of their brief to tell you anything connected with human feelings. This was an organisation that functioned smoothly but had no heart. Their counterparts at provincial and municipal levels appeared completely ignorant of what powers they had, and indeed seemed to have no freedom to exercise those powers. They simply passed on orders from above, while bitter experience meant that the staff who actually worked in the orphanages became more and more wary. None of them wanted to put a foot wrong and as result lose jobs working with foreigners, which were much coveted locally. The result was that, in 2006 and 2007, I found it more difficult than ever to get hold of information about adoption, in spite of the fact that China was supposed to have 'opened up' and 'modernised' with the reforms.

Just as I was starting to find it increasingly difficult to get verifiable and up-to-date information, I was fortunate to come across two very different women who worked in the adoption system.

I met one by chance, when she sat next to me on a flight from Auckland, New Zealand, to Sydney, Australia. She had just been to New Zealand to inspect adopting families, and her flight back to China meant changing planes in Sydney. As fellow Chinese passengers in foreign skies, we were immediately drawn together. To protect her identity, let us call her Wan. Wan was very young but, like a good government official, was extremely guarded in what she said. She had landed this job, with its regular foreign travel perks, because she was an English graduate.

Wan told me: 'The biggest headache for us is Americans who come in and film without permission. China's a country where the media is subject to controls. The Western media uses this footage of orphanages in poor areas as evidence to attack our government. The authorities crack down heavily on orphanages who get into the media spotlight. At the very least, they lose their funding, and in some cases, the whole staff is sacked and replaced, and they're stopped from sending children overseas for adoption. We get dragged in and criticised by the government too. All those foreigners think about is making a "historical record". They never consider Chinese people's feelings. If I were a girl adopted abroad, I wouldn't want people to know I had been picked up from some shambolic, godforsaken mountain village. It would be so humiliating!'

Wan was indignant. I was surprised that a top-level adoption worker could be so narrow-minded and suspicious of different cultures and customs. Surprised, also, that the deadly serious importance of 'face' in traditional Chinese culture was as deep-rooted as ever among the youth of today.

'Perhaps they feel they want their child to know what kind of background she came from, because it is part of the child's history,' I said, trying to make her understand.

'Well, that's *their* culture. How many Chinese people care about their origins?' She tried to justify her position. 'Change is happening so fast that they'll be too late to make a record of it anyway.'

If a young university graduate, I thought, felt like this about historical records in China, then what chance was there that small-town cadres who had had no higher education would appreciate local history and customs which went back thousands of years? 'It's just because change is happening so fast,' I said, 'that the parents want their child to have some record to keep of where they came from, after they've been adopted into a foreign country.'

'Of course, we all know that! But how many Chinese want their poverty-stricken home background shown up? You just told me you're from Shanghai and you grew up in Beijing. And these are both big cities so you can tell people, and it makes you sound very grand. But I'm from a small town in Shanxi province, and I'd never been to a big city until I went to university. For people like me from Shanxi, coal-mining towns such as Datong and Taiyuan seemed like the imperial capital; we really respected people who came from there. But when I got to Beijing and talked about Datong and Taiyuan, it was ridiculous. People looked at me as if I was a grimy-faced Datong coal miner – mostly they just sounded pitying! Those young girls who are going to grow up like princesses, will they really want to be reminded that they started out as Cinderellas?'

She was quite right about one thing: your place of origin and your accent at any level of Chinese society remain as important today, as a mark of status, as they ever were.

'I think,' I said, 'that as they grow up, their Western families will help them come to terms with the poverty of their backgrounds and birth parents. After all, they were born of Chinese mothers.'

But my arguments were lost on her: 'I think you've read too many books! Literature says one thing, but the truth is quite different. Mother love is supposed to be such a great thing, but so many babies are abandoned and it's their mothers who do it, isn't it! They're ignorant. They feel differently about emotions from the way you do. Where I come from, people talk about smothering a girl baby or just throwing it into the stream on the edge of the village to be eaten by dogs, as if it were a joke. How much do you think those women loved their babies?'

I was stung by her bluntness. 'They're surrounded by that kind of society. We all of us chat and laugh with people around us, at our work, by day. That's just so we can fit in, it makes life easier. But at night, or when we're alone, that's when we experience the feelings that no one else knows about, and we have to endure that on our own.'

She looked at me for a few seconds. She must have seen I was distressed and was kind-hearted enough not to want to hurt me, so she added: 'Yes, you're right, but still they don't have the education that you do, and they don't feel so much or so deeply.'

I was encouraged by the first part of her sentence but couldn't hold back my words. 'But human beings are the world's most "emotional" animals. Even losing something small that we like or value – a pen, a book, a bag – can make us feel pain and anxiety. Even a tiny child will cry if it drops an ice-cream on the ground. Imagine how much more a mother feels who has carried a baby in her womb for nine months, wondering all the time what that baby will be like. She can't stop herself thinking that, and she can't stop feeling pain either. Even in really dirt-poor areas, women will worry about a kitten or a puppy. So they're certainly going to feel real grief when their living baby girl is killed or taken from them.'

'You're obviously someone who really empathises with people,' she said. And I could tell she was not just trying to humour me. She really meant it. But she shook her head as she spoke. I could not believe her cynicism. Some of Wan's words came back to me later, when I heard Green Mary's story.

My eyes were drawn to the sea of clouds outside the aeroplane window, taking shape then dispersing for the whole of their existence. Children in many different cultures were taught to see clouds as beings that frolicked with the sun and the moon, shared humanity's joys and pain, and carried with them the dreams and hopes of so many women. Was this Chinese woman sitting beside me capable of feeling this gift of nature? Looking at the clouds, I said: 'I don't know. I just believe that maternal love is innate in any living creature. Maybe that love is not expressed in a way that we can understand, but I have absolutely no doubt that it has its own special means of expression. Uneducated mothers in poor Chinese villages have ways of loving

their children that we educated city-dwellers have never experienced and might not even recognise. One sad thing about
"modern" education and civilisation is that it only teaches us
to "feel" life through the experience of those who went before.
We have no way of communicating with other cultures naturally,
the way that animals naturally experience their surroundings
and other people . . .'

'Have you any proof of these notions of yours?' she asked,
looking past me out of the plane window.

'I spend a lot of time in villages,' I said, looking at her, 'and
I've had experience of the warmth and generosity of the old village
women.'

'It's certainly true that country people are much warmer than
city folk. City people are too concerned with competing for social
position, power and influence,' she said earnestly.

'Things should be much better now. I come back to China
often, but I never stay long so it's difficult to really get a feeling
for what's happening.' This was something I felt strongly about:
China was changing so fast, I felt a bit like a wild animal brought
up in captivity and then released into the wild – I would never
completely belong with my fellow creatures who had been born
and brought up in the wild.

*

Green Mary was the other adoption worker I met, Red Mary's
'disciple'. She said she had chosen that name in gratitude to Red
Mary. The women had worked together for two years and Green
Mary had made a written record of things like Westerners'
etiquette, the ways in which missionaries ran orphanages and
methods for rearing children in orphanages. Red Mary was aware
that she was getting on in years and should pass her knowledge
and experience on to the younger generation, so she encouraged
Green Mary and another young woman to record her experience
and put it into practice. But then the other woman went off with
a Spanish man who had come to adopt a baby, and Red Mary
was transferred to other work, and the project was not completed.

However, Green Mary had at least learned the basics of

orphanage management, and was intelligent enough to be able to build on this in her work. As result, she had been promoted to a senior position before she was forty. And it was she who told me one of the strangest and most curiously poignant stories that I heard – a morality tale for our work-obsessed times and one which made me question some of my own certainties.

Because she was now a government official I could not talk to her in her office, so we met in the Pure Lotus Vegetarian Restaurant, a business venture set up and run by Buddhist monks. Here, accompanied by the strains of Buddhist chants, we found a quiet corner to talk.

I explained to Green Mary why I wanted to speak to her: in order to help children adopted in the West to understand something of the lives of the birth mothers whom they would probably never meet, I was writing a book about Chinese women who gave up their babies.

'It's very difficult to get information about women who abandon their babies, and even harder to get them to tell you how they feel,' she said as she lowered herself decorously into one of the restaurant's soft sofas.

'You're absolutely right on that,' I said. Ever since I started to present live radio programmes at the end of the 1980s, I'd put all my efforts into learning how to get people to open up to me. It was very difficult, and I hadn't made much progress, but I kept trying. I'd approached it in all sorts of different ways and kept trying to get better at hearing what people were really saying to me. She saw that I was looking down at my fingernail.

'Your one red fingernail – is that part of being a good listener?' she asked suddenly, pointing at my finger.

Again she was right. And I told her about the bell pepper and my 'red spot'.

Green Mary looked thoughtful. 'But there are very few people like you who *want* to listen to women talk about their feelings,' she said softly. 'And for Chinese people, there are different kinds of feelings too. There are the kind of feelings that people like to talk about to other people, and then there are the things which people keep to themselves for their whole lives.'

I was silent. She had a point of course, but the burden of

keeping too many things to oneself could make the person ill. The suicide rate among Chinese women was high – and so many of those women had been driven to kill themselves by feelings they had kept to themselves.

When I did not say anything, Green Mary asked me another penetrating question: 'Apart from your work as a writer, do you have personal reasons for wanting to understand these mothers?' This woman had extraordinary antennae . . .

I answered without hesitation, and told her part of my own story. 'I'm a daughter with a mother and a father, but my parents and the rest of my family never really loved me, so I used to think my mother was actually my stepmother, like one of those children in stories. When I was older, I went to check, only to discover they were my real parents! I still can't understand why they sent me so far away to live with my paternal grandmother when I was just a month old. Did they really believe that dedicating themselves to the Revolution was more important than their own daughter? During the Cultural Revolution, our family of four ended up in three different places, either in detention or labour camps. My little brother and I were looked down on and humiliated, but to this day, our parents have never asked how we got through the experience. We were just two and a half and seven years old!

'Starting work and, especially, becoming a mother made me want to know what my parents really felt about me, their daughter. They only ever seemed interested in my career and my achievements. There's a generation gap, and our lives are different from theirs, but in my dreams I still want to be my mother's little girl, to hug her and have her hug me. I know I'm grown-up now, but she's still my mother, and I just can't stop missing her!'

Suddenly, all the feelings I had wanted to put into words came out, leaving me overwhelmed by the intensity of my emotions.

Green Mary leaned against the arm of the sofa and stared at me. She had lost her 'official' demeanour, and I could tell, from the look in her eyes, that there were emotions deeply felt by her that were just waiting to surface.

We were both silent for a while. She was obviously struggling to decide whether or not to open up to me. I wondered whether perhaps she had been a government official for too long, and it had become second nature to wall up her feelings.

Deciding that she would prefer to keep the conversation away from her own feelings at first, I went on: 'If you were my mother, what would you say to me? Would you blame it on the times we were living in, like everyone does? Is it really "the times" that make us do things? Those times are, after all, the history of people . . . I know there are lots of different answers, because everyone's different, but I want my mother to answer, as a mother . . .'

'Well, yes, that's probably what my own daughter wants from me too,' she said, more to herself than to me.

'Surely you're not working so hard that you can't spare any time for her?'

Amongst workers at any level in China, it was far too common for parents to be so busy that they neglected their children. Even though the government policy was for each family to have only one child, most children spent their lives either at school or doing homework. Read her a story? No time for that! Cook for him? No time for that! Play a game with her? No time for that either! They were all far too busy saving up for their toddler's university fees and marriage.

'I gave her away!' Those four words, spoken so quietly by her, came as a complete shock.

'You gave her away? You mean because you were an unmarried mother?' I did not understand. Why should a university graduate on a high salary like her need to give up her own daughter?

'No, it wasn't that. I discussed it with my husband and we agreed.' She spoke softly, the words coming out one by one, her eyes fixed on the teacup on the table in front of her.

'You mean you and your husband gave up your own daughter for adoption? How many children have you got, then?'

'Just the one.'

'Just her? Was it because she was a girl?'

'No, it wasn't that either.'

'Well, then . . .' I was bewildered.

'After we were married, I had several miscarriages and I was forty-two before I gave birth to a healthy baby. We adored her.

Our parents on both sides were dead so we had to get a nanny for her. But those *a-yis* from the countryside don't know what they're doing and I'd heard about so many near-disasters: once someone's daughter was stuffed into the washing machine, another time the *a-yi* let a two- or three-year-old run after the car, and one *a-yi* gave a baby pork lard to eat as a snack. One mishap after another! You know the kind of thing. But what else could we do?

'By day my husband and I worried ourselves sick, and at night we looked after her ourselves. My husband was over fifty. He got so tired he couldn't eat, and I was completely exhausted every day too. It was too awful. We were very busy at work, always getting back late and having to go to the office at weekends too. I had just been promoted and was responsible for the expansion of orphanages and overseas adoption, so I had to do a lot of travelling.

'My poor little girl, I felt so guilty. I just felt I'd let her down. Then one day I was visiting an orphanage in Sichuan, and someone reported one of the staff for passing her own child off as an orphan and putting her up for adoption. At the time, I thought, how could she do a thing like that? How could you give away your own flesh and blood? I called the girl in to see me. She was very junior, she did the cooking in the orphanage. She wept as she told me how hard life was for little girls in the mountains of Sichuan. Before they were five, they would be sent to work in the fields or up the mountain to get firewood which they had to bring down on their backs. She'd had a hard life herself. She had given her husband a son, but her in-laws wanted her to have another baby. They told her they would buy a Minority Nationality Birth Permit for her.*

'When she was pregnant with the second child, her in-laws pulled strings and got her a job as a cook in an orphanage in the town where her husband worked as a labourer. She saw the foreigners coming to pick up their new babies, and she realised that little girls could have a good life too, especially when they

---

* People of minority (non-Han Chinese) nationality in China are allowed to have more than one child. (*Trans.*)

sent back videos of their children's lives abroad. When she found out that she was going to have a girl, she bribed one of the staff to take her newborn baby away and put her on the adoption list. She was adopted by a French couple and they sent a video back to the orphanage. She saw the little girl living the life of a princess, and was happy for her, even though she missed her every day. Wasn't it better to know that she was having a good life than to suffer because her daughter was having a hard life?'

'So what she did put the idea into your head?' I guessed.

'It was like a light bulb coming on in my head. I let the cook off without punishing her, but I took her video back to Beijing with me. I watched it several times with my husband, and I was really moved by those parents – they used to read to their child every evening, and every time they had time off, they took her away on holiday. Eventually I convinced myself that it must be much better for a child to be adopted into a middle- or upper-class family in the West than to have to put up with a life in a society as fiercely competitive as ours. Besides, she'd be going abroad to study anyway when she was older.

'My husband and I must both have been cold-blooded creatures to do it, but partly it was because the opportunity arose. I gave her to an American couple, and I pulled strings to make sure my daughter didn't have to spend a single day in the orphanage. She was taken straight from home to their hotel!'

'Did you take her yourself?' I simply could not imagine how they had managed the transfer of their own little baby.

'How could I have done that?!' And she was silent for a long time. 'I arranged for an orphanage worker who didn't know me to pick her up from a small restaurant. The worker thought it was a child I had found. I made sure she videoed the adoptive parents for me. They were a kindly-looking middle-aged American couple. They held my daughter in their arms and were actually crying. My daughter seemed to understand their feelings, she patted the woman's face with her little hand and smiled at her, which made the woman cry even harder. Then they went into the hotel and the door shut on my daughter and her new family!'

She sank back exhausted in the sofa and said flatly: 'Were we very cruel?'

I did not know what to say. I wanted to scream at her, I wanted to weep for her little girl. Finally I said, 'I'm absolutely, absolutely sure you and your husband must have suffered a great deal after that.' I wanted to keep on repeating that 'absolutely'.

'We only realised what we had done when we got home. We came to our senses, but the nightmare had only just begun. The peace and quiet in our house was nothing like before she was born. Photographs of her, her clothes, her toys, all lying in a heap . . . it felt like they were digging a great hole in my heart. I missed her so much. To be perfectly honest, we neither of us could help ourselves, we sneaked into the hotel where the couple were staying that evening. We heard her crying and crying as soon as we got to the floor where their room was. She was calling "Ma-ma, ma-ma" and her voice was choked with sobs. I'd never heard her cry like that before. My husband was afraid I'd burst into the room and take her back, so he grabbed me by the arm. Yes, I really would have done if he hadn't got hold of me! We didn't leave until security did their night-time rounds and asked us what we were doing.

'We didn't eat dinner after we got home, we just sat down on the sofa. We sat there all night. About eight o'clock the next morning, he said he was going to buy a newspaper. I watched him go out and for the first time, I really hated him. How did he have the heart to read the newspaper?! While he was gone, I took a taxi back to the hotel and sat in the corner of the coffee bar, hoping I would see her.

'It was nearly midday when the couple came down with my daughter. She was facing towards me, but too far away to see me. She was looking blankly ahead, into the unknown . . . Then she was carried out to a coach. My heart was pounding, but it was no good, my legs just wouldn't move. Eventually I got up and went towards the coach, but suddenly my husband was at my side, pinning me to him! The coach slowly pulled away – and I slid to the ground almost in a faint. One of the hotel security staff came and enquired politely whether I was all right and what relationship we were to each other. He said my husband had been wandering around the hotel since about eight in the morning!'

Light suddenly dawned. 'He never went to buy a newspaper, after all, just to see your daughter,' I said.

'Yes. And from that day until our divorce, he never spoke a single word to me. Everything was written down on a little kitchen blackboard. He blamed me for being cold-blooded and not fit to be a mother. Though he had agreed to our plan. We took the decision together. But what's the use in going over it now? We both knew after our daughter was adopted that it was finished between us.

'Not a minute goes by without me thinking of her. Sometimes if I see a coach starting up, I fantasise that she's on it. I pile her toys by me on the bed and spend the nights half awake, half dreaming. If I wasn't so crazily busy at work, it would drive me mad. It hurts too much to think about her – I'd really go mad!'

I asked if she had any news of the little girl.

'Last year on her fifth birthday, the orphanage got a video from the parents. The candles on the cake were lit, and she was facing the camera, making a wish: "I want my Chinese mummy to know that I'm a good girl!"' Green Mary's voice was choked with tears.

One of the monk waiters came over, gave the Buddhist greeting with joined hands and put a pile of paper napkins on the table. Then he said quietly, 'Has the bitter draught of tears brought you to an understanding?' When neither of us responded, he went away.

'You said you want to ask your mother so many questions, Xinran,' she went on. 'On that video, my daughter asked her own question: "I want to know why my Chinese mummy didn't want me. Was it because I was a bad girl?"' And she broke down in sobs again.

I could scarcely contain myself. I wanted to ask her the same question! 'Why? *Why?*' Just how 'civilised' were we becoming? What was education and work really for? And all this struggling to compete and to succeed, at what price? Why had our modern civilisation discarded that ancient blind animal instinct to protect our young? My books have come out in dozens of different languages all over the world, and I have received emails and videos from adopting families all over the world. The question most often asked is precisely that one: 'Why didn't my Chinese mummy want me?'

Green Mary saw my look of indignation, and said in a small voice, 'Lots of people think I gave my daughter to relatives to bring up, and am dedicating myself to adoption work. No one knows that the reason I work like crazy is because of my own daughter and other little girls like her!'

'Have other parents done the same as you in other orphanages?' I wanted to know, expecting the answer 'no'.

'You want the honest truth?' She looked at me with some anxiety.

'Of course.' I gave her what I felt was a very firm look.

'It will only be one bit of your research, won't it? I hope there won't be trouble if I tell you . . . Yes, there are lots of orphanage workers who help their relatives in the countryside "abandon" their babies, and get them adopted,' she said with some hesitation.

'People working in orphanages help other people abandon their babies? It's against nature! And you mean people like you not only don't put a stop to it, you actually direct it? Has that become standard procedure?' I felt she should not shirk her own responsibility for this.

She flared up at this. 'What's nature? What's mother love? What standard? Who's the standard modelled on? You've been to these villages? You've seen what pitiful lives village girls lead? They only survive at all by good luck! I don't insist on the "standard" if those girls can go to Western families and live happy, healthy lives and get excellent schooling . . . That's so much better than them suffering the same sad fate that their mothers did, or even worse. They'll be valued emotionally and physically a thousand times more if they're adopted abroad.'

'But it leaves a black hole in the mother's heart, and unanswered questions in the daughter's –'

She cut me short: 'Chinese women are the most unselfish in the world. They'll do anything for their husbands and children, suffer any pain, shed their own blood and tears to look after them! The one thing that comforts them is that one day their daughters may understand that their mothers loved them, and that they paid for that love with an endless stream of bitter tears!'

'Do you really believe that those daughters can understand how much their mothers gave and what it cost them?'

'I am quite sure that when they go through the pain of pregnancy and childbirth and become mothers themselves, it will make them understand what a mother's love is.'

'And the round-the-clock feeding, changing and rocking the new baby to sleep may give them a taste of the hardships their birth parents suffered,' I added.

'Of course. That's why I always say to people involved in adoption work that Chinese mothers should never think that their daughters belong to them alone. The birth parents brought those babies into this world, but the adopting parents have given them their present life!'

*

After I had said goodbye to Green Mary that day, my thoughts turned again to Red Mary. What would she have said if she had heard the other Mary's story? One of the women was an abandoned baby, the other a mother who had deliberately abandoned her baby. By some quirk of fate, they had both ended up dedicating their lives to orphanage work and to those abandoned baby girls.

9

Bonds of Love: Stones and Leaves

The Sun God had a beloved daughter, Nüwa, so beautiful that the Yellow Emperor himself was full of praise for her.

FOR MANY years now, I have carried with me a scrap of dried leaf or a particular pebble as I travel round the world. These came to me from a mother and a young girl who lived on the banks of China's Yangtze River.

The 'pebble mother' lived in what was then the town of Fengdu, at the western end of the navigable reaches of the Yangtze River, not far from the city of Chongqing, with its population of 30 million. Fengdu was a town which, for centuries, had been known as 'home' not just to an earthly populace, but to heavenly spirits and the ghosts of the Underworld.*

I first met the pebble mother in 1984, before I started as a radio presenter but when I was already doing some freelance journalism. We had been to Chengdu on a work trip and were making a detour to the Yangtze on our way back to Beijing. We

---

* Fengdu was an ancient town perched on a hillside overlooking the upper reaches of the Yangtze River on the south-eastern edge of the Sichuan basin. Known as Bazi Biedu during the spring and autumn period (second half of the eighth century BC to the first half of the fifth century BC), it had a famous necropolis dating back over 1,800 years, modelled on the Hell of Taoist mythology. Fengdu was the 'ghost capital' of China, and was an extraordinarily atmospheric place, rich in historical and cultural associations. Indeed it is described in such famous supernatural tales as *Journey to the West, Strange Stories from a Chinese Studio, Complete Tales of Yue Fei* and *The Story of Zhong Kui*. However, with the completion of the Three Gorges Dam it was swallowed up by the rising waters, although the scenery above the 'Door of Hell' has remained above the water level. Its living population, meanwhile, has been moved to New Fengdu, whose white-tiled buildings line the opposite bank.

decided to take one of the long-distance steamers downstream and enjoy the scenery in what was still a largely undeveloped region. The steamers were at that time the main means of transport for the local population. We took a passenger steamer which plied its way downstream, stopping to let passengers on and off by day, and take on water and supplies by night. The long evening stopovers also gave us the opportunity to visit some of the villages on the river banks.

Economic reforms had not yet filtered down from the big cities to these poor fishing villages, and the local population existed on whatever the heavens, the mountains and the waters bestowed on them. There were scarcely any modern manufactured goods to be seen at all. The villagers lived in primitive huts made of bamboo and grass and, for clothes, wore traditional capes made from coir to keep off the rain, trousers and a bamboo hat, supplemented, for the women, by a piece of cloth which covered their chests. The children ran around them naked. Government restrictions didn't reach this far or to these peasants whose family life was based on labour. Here, the one-child policy was not implemented because life was harsh, few children survived to adulthood and even girls were useful.

The huts were almost bare of furniture, and the villagers' diet consisted of wild greens, fish and rice mixed together and stuffed into a tube of hollow bamboo. This was cooked over a fire and then split open lengthways ready for eating. A small piece of salted vegetable or a little salt would be added, and you held the split-open tube in one hand and, with the other, shovelled the food into the mouth with a utensil made of a long strip of bamboo. Food cooked in a bamboo tube always tasted light and fresh. This was the normal evening meal for villagers living along the middle reaches of the Yangtze, and this was what we ate every evening too. To add flavour, the better-off added oil and vegetables, and the poorest added tiny fish or shrimps which they had caught during the day and which were too small to sell.

Modern habits had had no impact on their way of life: dinners were eaten by the whole family together, and were the chief social activity. Visitors were a rarity so were a great event for everyone, and the whole village, young and old alike, would sit around the cooking fire with the visitor talking, laughing and eating. That was the grandest way in which they could entertain their guests, and the tips left by the latter were their chief source of income.

One evening, I remember that we had just visited the Fengdu ghost town, and the steamer was tied up at a tiny jetty at the water's edge. We had been dragged off to the local fishing village for a bamboo tube dinner. The flames from the cooking fire caught the ripples on the water's surface, looking sometimes like stars, sometimes like a stream of light, or a bunch of mischievous sprites wanting to play games. This was a fairy place, and the outlines of the distant mountain slopes provided a mysterious backdrop of velvety blackness. The air was permeated with the scent of the bamboo leaves and the smell of fish. As a city-dweller, I had never seen night scenery like this. I sat there, absorbing, little by little, the peacefulness of my surroundings.

As I looked at the dark shapes of the distant mountains, I suddenly saw a slender figure sitting on a rock which jutted out into the waters of the river. The figure kept moving, as if he or she were throwing something into the water. Whatever was it? A spirit, a fairy . . . ? It made me think of that haunting Chinese myth of Jingwei who tries to fill up the sea with twigs and pebbles.

*

The Sun God had a beloved daughter, Nüwa, so beautiful that the Yellow Emperor himself was full of praise for her.

When the Sun God was not at home, Nüwa played on her own. However, she longed for her father to take her on his journeys to the East Sea where the sun rises. The Sun God, however, was busy every day directing the sun's course from its rising every morning until its setting at night, and could not take his daughter along. One day Nüwa secretly rowed after him in a boat, but unfortunately a storm arose and mountainous waves capsized the small craft. Nüwa was swallowed up by the cruel sea, never to return. Her father was grief-stricken – unable to harness the sun's rays to shine on her and bring her back to life, he was left alone to mourn his loss.

However, Nüwa was then reborn as a bird with a striped head, red claws and a white beak. She was given the name Jingwei, from her plaintive cry of 'jingwei, jingwei . . .'

Jingwei could not forgive the cruel sea for snatching away her young life, and vowed to take revenge. She would fill in the sea and make it into dry land. She began to pick up pebbles in her beak, flying back and forth between her home on Fajiu Mountain and the East Sea. Over and over again she made the journey, carrying one pebble or twig at a time, circling above the choppy waves and calling plaintively, then dropping in whatever she had brought.

The sea surged and thundered, pouring scorn on her efforts. 'Little bird,' it said. 'Give up! Even if you work for a million years, you'll never make me into a flat plain!' But Jingwei answered from high in the air: 'Even if it takes me ten million or a hundred million years, till the end of the world, I'll fill you in and make you dry land!'

'Why do you hate me so much?' asked the sea.

'Because you stole my young life and you will do the same to other innocent young people. I'll carry on for as long as it takes to finish my work!'

And up she flew again, calling 'jingwei, jingwei', and headed back to Fajiu Mountain to fetch more pebbles and twigs. Back and forth she flew tirelessly, dropping more and more into the sea. The months and years went by until one day a sea swallow came by. He was nonplussed – what was the other bird doing? But when he had heard her story, he was moved by her dogged persistence. They married and hatched a fine brood of chicks – the males took after their sea swallow father, while the females followed their mother, Jingwei, and joined her in her interminable task of fetching pebbles and twigs to fill up the sea.

Chinese people greatly respect Jingwei for her selflessness, her stubborn determination and bold ambition. The Jin dynasty poet Tao Yuanming celebrated this little bird's brave struggle against the ocean waves in verse, and her story has become a byword for magnificent idealism and arduous endeavour.

The admiration of ordinary people for Jingwei can be seen in the numerous memorials to her, bearing such names as 'Jingwei makes a vow to the waters' and 'Jingwei fills the sea' which can still be seen up and down the eastern seaboard of China.

*

I asked a fisherman sitting at the fireside: 'Who is that?'

'That's a madwoman. She comes here every evening to feed her daughter,' he answered casually.

I did not understand him, though I thought of Jingwei. But the silhouetted figure was really not far off, and my companions were busy playing 'fish heads'* with the villagers, so I quietly left them and went over to her.

The silhouette had heard me coming and, without looking round, said: 'I'm not mad. I come here to see my daughter.' She had obviously overheard my question and the fisherman's answer. She spoke much better *putonghua* (standard Chinese) than the other locals.

'Where is your daughter?' I asked, looking around. I could see nothing.

'In the river!' She still did not look at me.

Her words made me think she really might be mad.

'Mum says my big sister was taken away by the river,' a little voice piped up from her mother's arms.

I quietly came closer to the figure. In the pale moonlight, it was hard to make her out clearly. I did not want to disturb them and simply sat down beside them. If my companions by the fire wanted me, they would surely see that my silhouette had joined hers, I thought.

'Mum, can I see my big sister?' A small hand emerged and pointed at the river in the moonlight.

'Yes, when you're big, you can go out on a boat and see her,' the shadow mother answered.

'Will you go with me?' The hand retreated again.

---

* The fisherfolk keep the fish heads after selling the bigger fish to the large boats, and play games with them: they stand one each on a single chopstick or a twig and wait to see whose falls over first; or attach a fish head to something and spin it around – when it stops, whoever the mouth is pointing at must sing a song or do a turn or have a drink; and there are other games too in different areas.

'Yes, providing I'm not too old to get around! The shadow cuddled the child to her.

'But why don't you go and see my big sister now?' a small head poked out and asked.

'Mum's got to look after your granny and grandpa. If we went away, then what would they do without us?' The shadow pressed her head tightly against her child's.

'Then cook them lots and lots of bamboo tubes and they'll be all right.' The little hand patted the shadow's head.

'The weather's so hot, they'll go off and start to smell.' The shadow dropped a kiss on the child's head.

'Then we'll go in winter,' and the hand pointed again at the river.

'If we don't chop firewood and do the planting in winter, what will Granny and Grandpa eat?'

'But we won't ever find my sister just sitting here every day.' The child struggled to one side and took hold of her mother's face with both hands.

The shadow mother said nothing, but just threw something that looked like a bamboo food tube into the river.

'What's your mum throwing into the river?' I asked the small hands moving in the moonlight.

'Food in bamboo tubes. She says that the fish will eat them and then my sister will eat the same as us.'

'Where did your sister go?'

'She was kidnapped!' the child answered simply, as if she did not know the meaning of what she was saying.

I was horrified.

'Kidnapped,' the shadowy figure repeated heavily. 'I had left her on the shore just for a moment. But I was too late to save her. With my own eyes, I saw two men grab her, run to the boat and then they were gone. Oh, why was I too late?'

'People-traffickers here?' I asked.

'They often snatch children and sell them, I know that,' she said. (They were sold to peasants and fishermen downriver for labour and later to become their wives.) 'It was a very windy day and the water was choppy. I thought they might not make it to the shore. What a sin! My poor little girl, she lost her mother when she was just six months old. She'll be five now, she must be up the mountain chopping firewood already! I wish I knew if she was getting enough to eat.' The shadow's voice was full of remorse.

Her words chilled me. I did not yet know what it felt like to be a mother, but the pain in that woman's voice would haunt me for years after that.

Before our boat left the next day, when we were taking pictures of the sunrise from the river bank, a little girl of five or six danced up to me and held out her hand. In it was a milky white bean-shaped pebble. 'My mum says if you see my big sister please give her this, so she won't be hungry!'

As we set off, I saw the child holding the hand of a woman so weighed down with firewood that she almost completely disappeared under it. They stood together watching, the woman still carrying her burden, as the boat sailed on round the peak. In the last glimpse I had of them, the little girl still seemed to be waving. I held the pebble in my hand, remembering the child's words: 'My mum says if my big sister has this, she won't be hungry!'

Could you eat pebbles? I knew the mother did not mean that. She must have missed her daughter so badly and just wanted to be able to get something to her, wherever she might be. She believed that if her daughter saw the pebble her mother had sent her, she might not miss her mother so much. But who was her daughter, and where was she now?

*

My scrap of dried leaf, on the other hand, came from Jiujiang on the lower reaches of the Yangtze, some years later. I passed through Jiujiang on a work trip in 1996. As I stepped on to the river bank, I saw a girl of fourteen or fifteen staggering along the road laden down by a heavy load of small pottery birds. I walked along behind her wondering if I should give her a hand, although to be honest, I did not know how. I certainly did not want to risk breaking any of her little birds. It was only when she paused for breath that I realised what a tiny thing she was. Then a woman came up and gave her 50 cents, and the girl put her burden down.

Inquisitively, I asked, 'Where are you going?'

'To the next job!' she said, not looking at me, but carefully stuffing her money away through an opening at the neckline of her jacket.

'What kind of job?' I asked.

Now she looked at me and said seriously, 'Portering. Why do you ask? I live here, my family's here too.'

'Do you go to school? You don't look sixteen years old!' I looked her up and down.

'I'm just fifteen. I did two years of school, then we couldn't afford it any more,' she said glumly, and set off at a brisk pace towards the river.

I had plenty of time, so I decided to carry on chatting to the girl.

'Isn't there anything else you can do? This is a job for a boy!'

'You have to work fixed hours with other jobs. My dad's at home ill, and I have to keep an eye on him. With this work I can come and go as I please, and the pay's not bad.'

'Do you live far from here?'

'Not far.' She pointed to a group of shacks on the river embankment.

'Can you take me there? I'll pay you, as good a price as portering,' I said, getting my purse out.

'Don't you go cheating me. Everyone knows me around here, in this town and around about,' she warned me.

'I won't cheat you. I'd just like to know how you and your family live. I'm a broadcaster, I talk on the radio.'

'Really? Around here, we often listen to the radio being broadcast in the street. There's a lot of that goes on. So how do I know you're not going to cheat me?'

'Okay, let me show you my Press Card.'

'I can't read, I can only do a bit of adding and taking away,' she said, not bothering to look at the card in my hand.

'Okay, let me think, then . . . I'll give you 50 yuan up front.* You take that now, and have my watch as well. If I cheat you, you can break my watch.' I undid my watch strap.

---

* Fifty yuan in the 1990s was about equivalent to 500 yuan ($73/£44) today (2009).

'That would be such a pity. I couldn't take it. If I broke it, I couldn't pay you for it. Don't worry, I believe you. This money is more than I earn in a week!'

As she took me to her house, the girl told me her name was Ye'r, which means 'leaf'. Before her mother died, she had told her daughter she was a girl 'without roots', because the family had bought her. It was not only passenger and goods transport that flourished on the Yangtze River – there was a flourishing trade in stolen goods and in people too. There were not nearly enough river police and launches to put a stop to it. Besides, many of the police were gang members too. According to Ye'r, the locals made no distinction between the police and the traffickers. Everyone in her town joined the gangs, and members helped and protected each other. Outsiders were kept out and any who did turn up were 'terminated'. I was surprised to hear such a young girl talking about her community in such an adult way.

Ye'r's house was not far from the town, on the river embankment. Not that you could really call it a house, as it was just a thatched hut. Inside, someone was fast asleep on a wooden board, his legs covered in flies. Ye'r went in and quietly shooed them off him. There was no reaction from the man and she came out again, indicating to me that I should sit down on the landing stage made of wooden piles at the water's edge.

Ye'r looked back at the hut: 'I don't think he'll last much longer. His legs are all rotting.'

'Why haven't you taken him to the hospital?' I asked.

'He won't let me get help. He says he doesn't want a doctor. There's a very kind doctor in the town who wanted to help him, but he won't let him,' Ye'r said flatly.

'Why?' I pursued.

'He says it's retribution, he's getting what he deserves.' Ye'r pressed her lips together.

'What retribution?' I asked. Life really was full of surprises – you never knew what was coming round the next corner.

'Both my mother and father used to work on a boat, collecting rubbish from the river banks, and carrying people and goods. They stole me as a baby, he told me that after he fell ill. Before my mother died she said I had been bought, but my dad said she never told the truth right up till when she died, so she'd end up as a water ghost.'

'And did he tell you where your birth parents were?' Her words made me think of the shadowy figures of mother and daughter I had met twelve years before, and the little pebble they had given me. But on this trip I had not brought my pebble with me.

'Yes, six months ago he told me everything,' she answered casually.

'So? Didn't you go off and find them?' I found it hard to imagine how she could have restrained her anger.

'And what would my dad have done without me? Who would have looked after him?' Ye'r looked puzzled.

I was moved by her kindness. 'And when he dies, do you think you'll go?'

'I'd like to, but will my mother recognise me? So many children are stolen, how will I ever find out who I am?'

'Ask your father again. I'm sure he could tell you a few details which would convince your birth mother you're her daughter,' I said encouragingly.

'My father says it's very likely she's died.' Ye'r looked down.

'Why?' I bent my head close to hers.

Ye'r looked at the river: 'He said that before I was stolen, my mother was known for miles around as the beauty of the Yangtze upper reaches, but a few years ago someone pointed her out to him, and she looked so old she was almost unrecognisable.'

'Do you know why?' I asked her, though I thought I knew the answer.

'My dad said it was probably because of the sin they had done to her.' She turned to look at me.

'Do you think she missed her baby?' I thought again of the shadow woman.

'I don't know.' She looked uncertain.

'And you really haven't thought about going to see her?' I pursued.

Ye'r was defensive. 'I didn't know anything about it when I was little. I only found out six months ago when he got ill. He told me because he was afraid he'd turn into a water ghost, too!'

'So do you hate your parents?' Surely she must hate them, I thought.

'Why would I do that?' was the response.

'Because they snatched you away from your birth mother, of course!'

To my surprise, Ye'r said earnestly, 'Well, I don't hate them. I never knew my birth mother, and now I do know about her but I have no idea what she's like. Besides, my mum and dad never beat me, and around here there isn't a family where the daughters don't get beaten and sworn at, but they never did that to me.'

Before I left that day, I divided all the money I had on me into two and gave Ye'r an extra 25 yuan. She tried to refuse it, saying that it was like stealing to take money for doing nothing. Finally I persuaded her to take it by saying she should keep it for when she could take a boat trip to find her birth mother.

We spent the night on board our steamer at its moorings in the little town but I did not sleep. I was thinking about Ye'r, the girl whose new parents had committed an evil deed in kidnapping her, and yet had treated her so kindly.

The next day, Ye'r came to see us off. She put a little package wrapped in the leaf of a tree into my hand. I opened it to find a smaller greenish-yellow leaf inside. 'I don't own anything at all,' she said. 'But if you go upstream and see my birth mother, please give her this leaf and it'll make her pretty again!'

I was struck dumb by her words. I thought back to the pebble and the shadow mother who had said, 'Please give her this, so she won't be hungry!' I wished I had brought her pebble with me. Now Ye'r wanted me to give the leaf to the mother she had never known, so that she would be pretty again. What made them so sure that I would meet their loved ones? Was it simply a coincidence? Or had the spirit of the river got into me?

I often put the pebble and the leaf together after that, feeling somehow that it allowed the mother to embrace her daughter.

And that was the reason, when I left China, I managed to squeeze the pebble and the leaf into my suitcase, although I could not have said exactly why I felt unable to leave them behind. When I started work on *The Good Women of China*, I felt as if

I were taking the first steps towards finding out. And later when, in 2004, I set up The Mothers' Bridge of Love, I knew I had arrived at the answer: that pebble and that leaf represented those millions of mothers who never saw their daughters again; they were my way of bringing a message and a loving embrace to all those daughters who have never known their mothers.

10

Little Snow, Where Are You?

'She's so small, poor little thing, and sending her to an orphanage would upset even the spirits of her dead parents!'

I HAVE MY own very special secret. It is something I hardly ever talk about but it is the reason why I have tried so hard to bring mothers and daughters together.

Once I fostered a little girl. Her name was Xue'r.

She was born at the end of 1990 but it was a difficult birth and, sadly, her mother haemorrhaged and died when Xue'r was only three days old. Although the mother had not even had a chance to put her daughter to the breast, she did give her the name Xue'r ('Little Snow'), after the great snowflakes which had floated down outside the window on the day she was born like so many fairies bringing the child into the world. There was something else too – on the baby's forehead was a dark pink birthmark, etched into her skin, according to the hospital nurses, by a tear the dying mother shed as she held her daughter in her arms . . .

Her parents had been deeply in love, and after his wife died, the husband, a surgeon, had taken large quantities of sleeping pills, slashed himself twice with a scalpel, and had lain down to die next to his wife in the hospital mortuary. He left a very simple farewell note: he could not leave his beloved wife alone and lonely in the Underworld. About his daughter, Little Snow, he said not a word.

I was at the hospital interviewing people who had been

injured in a snowstorm when a nurse told me this beautiful but tragic tale. I decided to go and see the little orphan. Little Snow lay quietly in a cot in the empty children's ward. Whether by accident or design, the nurses had put her by the window and as the snowflakes floated down, the shadows they made on the baby's face seemed like the tears of the mother who had left her baby behind. Looking at her, I felt tears come to my own eyes.

I picked up and kissed the baby's little pink 'teardrop mark', hoping that she would feel that someone else apart from her mother loved her. Little Snow opened her bright eyes and seemed to look into mine. The nurse said that neither side of the family wanted her because she was a girl, and so the hospital would have to send her to an orphanage.

On my way home, Little Snow kept coming back into my mind. As soon as it was light the next morning, I made my way to the hospital through the whirling snow. The nurses on duty told me that she would be taken to the orphanage that afternoon, when the weather had improved. I found the staff nurse, and said I wanted to foster Little Snow. She looked at me and said, 'Xinran, you can't rush into something like this. Never mind all the procedures to be gone through – and I doubt they'd accept you – there'd be problems when the child's due to start school. Besides, you already have a child, so you wouldn't be allowed to adopt another under the one-child policy!'

'But – if I just foster her?' I begged. 'It'll reduce the burden on the state.'

'You're not trying to reduce the burden on the state, you're feeling sorry for the child!' said the staff nurse brusquely but accurately.

'Well, yes, you're right,' I admitted. 'She's so small, poor little thing, and sending her to an orphanage would upset even the spirits of her dead parents!'

'Of course it would. We're all human, we all have feelings. But the hospital has never done anything like this. How can we let you foster her? Only the grandparents have the right to foster, even uncles and aunts aren't allowed to. The family planning authorities would worry about setting a precedent. The relatives of couples who have "extra" babies might want to adopt them! We can't do it! We'd get into trouble!'

I tried another tack and asked her: 'So where do I go if I want to apply to foster her legally?'

'Well, I've never heard of it happening before, no one's ever asked to do what you want to do. We can't help you.'

I could see that the staff nurse, like so people at middle management level in China, would never take a decision on her own account. She merely transmitted orders from the upper to the lower ranks, a functionary, not a human being. So I went to see someone higher up in the hospital, who was an old friend of mine. He made a wise suggestion: I should take her home now, while Little Snow was still down in the hospital records as their patient. In a couple of months it would be Chinese New Year, and policy might change or be relaxed. When that time came, we would all try and find a way through this.

And that was how Little Snow became my daughter. My son Panpan was one and a half years old, and was just learning to walk and talk. He used to muddle up the names 'Mama' (Mum) and 'Meimei' (little sister), and when Little Snow cried, hushed her the way I did with him, saying 'Mama, meimei, mama, meimei'. Our *a-yi* at that time was a good-looking young woman and it was not surprising that as Little Snow grew prettier by the day, rumours started to go round that she was our *a-yi*'s illegitimate daughter!

With us, Little Snow got plenty of food and good care; she quickly grew plump and turned into a strong, active baby, quite a heavy bundle to carry around. Nearly three months passed and it was Chinese New Year. People came to the house to wish us a Happy New Year and all fell under the spell of my lively daughter's happy smiles.

I was extremely naïve in those days. I really thought that by some devious means I could manage to adopt Little Snow, that I could find loopholes in a policy which grew stricter by the day, that I was surrounded by people willing to help me, and that I could give Little Snow a real family. How wrong I was. Straight after the Chinese New Year, the head of the radio station came to see me for a private chat: he advised me to give up Little Snow.

Not long after that, I was warned by Personnel that if I did not act soon, the head might lose his job as well as me, because I had disobeyed the one-child family planning policy. This was equivalent to taking a colleague's dinner bowl away from him, because it was the workplace which administered the almost military-style rationing system of those days, and if you were thrown out of your job, you were unlikely to be able to find another. You could not even go and farm the land.

I had no choice but to give in; at least, to agree outwardly. I held off for as long as I could, on the pretext of getting together her things and her medical records. I prayed for a miracle, I hoped that somehow my Little Snow would be forgotten. However, the family planning officers were intransigent, and less than two weeks later the station head came to see me again, and gave me a written warning that I would be disciplined. My offence would remain on my records for the rest of my life!

'Xinran,' he said gloomily, 'if you don't want to give the baby up, that's your business. But if they kick you out, we'll suffer the consequences too. At the very least, I'll be demoted. Family planning and the one-child policy is a national policy, not a local government policy that's flexible. I do hope you'll spare a thought for those of us who'll share the responsibility . . .'

At this, I knew I really had no choice. It was not only that my boss and friend was going to be dragged into this, and that I would lose my job. It was the fact that I would no longer be able to provide for my children at the most basic level. And Little Snow would be regarded as an 'illegal' for the rest of her life. That was not fair on her.

Once I knew I would have to give up Little Snow, sleep deserted me and I began to look drawn and miserable. In the three months or so that she had been with us, Little Snow had come to depend on me for her happiness; she trusted me the way any child trusts its mother.

The day before Little Snow was to leave, I put the heating on and made the flat cosy and warm. Then I tried on her every piece of clothing I had bought for her for the following summer, autumn, winter and spring. I had bought them with plenty of room for growth so our little three-month-old looked quite ridiculous in her summer outfits (intended for an eight-month baby) and her winter outfits (for twelve months), but the *a-yi* and I could not raise a smile. We held back the tears as we changed her from one garment to another, imagining as we did so how she would look when she was bigger. Then we worked till late at night packing her bags.

The next day we all went with Little Snow to the hospital. I comforted myself and the *a-yi* by saying that we could go and see her in the orphanage, and she would always be our Little Snow.

It was a long and agonising week before I managed to sneak away and see Little Snow, without daring to tell anyone where I was off to. It took me nearly three hours of searching – in a city which was under constant reconstruction – before I found the orphanage, not far from the city centre. I could hardly believe the evidence of my eyes: was this rudimentary shack made of brick and wood really an orphanage? An old woman kindling a fire outside the low wooden door motioned me silently in. The door was battered, and the room inside small – just a dozen square feet. To the right was a stove; in the corner, a few bowls, chopsticks and kitchen utensils; against the wall facing the door was a primary school desk with, next to it, an adult-size single bed; tucked into the left-hand corner, there was a shelf made of wooden slats and shaped like wide desk drawers, which held the babies. The smallest had room to spare, but the heads and feet of the biggest touched the wall or the wooden edge! There were nine of them altogether and almost all were dressed in Little Snow's clothes.

I caught my breath, aghast. Was my Little Snow there too? Suddenly I saw her. It had been only a week but she had grown much thinner. Her little face was wan and her lively expression was gone. She must have been too hungry for any energetic wriggling. She actually recognised me, and held out her little arms as if in protest at being abandoned here! I was utterly stricken. I picked her up and burst into floods of tears. Of course, my crying terrified the other infants and they set up accompanying wails.

Thinking back on it, we must have sounded more solemn and tragic than Beethoven's Fifth Symphony! The old nurse came in at the noise, and introduced herself as Mother Tang. Wiping the tears from her own eyes, Mother Tang told me the following story:

'We can't do anything. The government has no money, and we don't get support from anyone. It's hard enough just to keep the children alive. Lucky we had those clothes from you, they've kept the cold draughts off the other babies. If I light a coal fire in the room, I'm afraid the fumes will make them ill, but the way it is now, I'm afraid the cold will be the death of them.'

'What about officials from the local government, haven't they paid a New Year visit?' My reporter's instincts reasserted themselves.

'They said they'd come, but then some more important government business came up, and they didn't turn up. The person who brought the message said this place is due for demolition, the orphanage will be moved and things should get better after that. But no one's been by since then, except for the wages clerk at the beginning of the month.' Mother Tang busied herself with pouring out the children's rice gruel.

'Haven't any of you complained?' I always tried to make other people into reporters too, because I felt everyone should take responsibility for telling the authorities what was really happening.

'Who to? Before, we had someone who knew what to say and could write letters, but now the orphanage has been turned into a business. No one wants to come here and there's only me left, and a woman from the countryside. She's out shopping. I ask you, look at what hunger's doing to these kids. We're just not given enough food for them. They suck it down with all their might, and won't let go of the bottle until they've had every last drop!'

'Do the relatives come and see them?' I quickly got the milk powder I had brought with me out of my bag.

'That's wonderful!' she exclaimed in delight, before continuing: 'These girls are so lucky to have Little Snow here. They're orphans – who's going to come and see them? The families can't get rid of them quick enough. If anyone does come, it's only to ask if we have any boys. Haven't you noticed every single one of them's a girl? It's such a worry, they get bigger every day, and what are we to do with them then . . . ?'

'What happened to them in the past?' Selfishly I gave one of the bottles of formula to Little Snow first.

'I don't know,' she said, feeding one of the smallest babies. 'This orphanage is temporary, an overflow annexe added on when the old one was full. But the local government had nowhere to house it. I don't know where they got this place from. I used to work in a kindergarten until I retired and I was sitting at home with nothing to do. My old man died years ago and the children have flown the nest. Luckily I can still get around so I can look after the children, poor little things. The country woman does the night shift and she's very capable. She got rid of a baby daughter and couldn't have a son, so her husband threw her out. She looks after these children like her own daughter. She's very reliable, but we just don't have the money to buy them food and clothes, they grow so fast, and the four seasons are so different around here. We can't keep up . . .'

That night, when I had finished the programme and gone home, I turned out every cupboard and drawer and got out every single item of Panpan's clothing, the light summer things and the warm winter outfits. I kept just two changes of clothes for him. Then I packed up all the bedding except for one spare set. The next morning, as soon as the banks opened, I went and got out some money (we did not have ATMs in those days) and went back to the orphanage with two large carry-bags. We three women laid the bedding out on the slats to make them a bit warmer. Then I sent Mother Tang out to buy some milk products and a couple of hanging mobiles for the children. They needed bright colours and sounds to listen to! Back at the radio station I looked out a big pile of address cards of friends and wrote to each of them appealing for help.

Two responded immediately, offering support. One was the head of a furniture factory, offering ten cots for up to twelve-year-olds, and a playpen. The other was the director of a milk products factory, offering to deliver fresh milk free every day. The only condition was that I should mention their generosity on my daily programme.

I felt comforted as I saw that dark, lifeless orphanage transformed into a brighter, more cheerful place. Mother Tang, and her assistant who had not said a word so far, cheered up too. I hoped that all these improvements would offer some consolation to the assistant, who must be grieving for her own daughter.

I did not dare to share any of the goings-on connected with Little Snow with my colleagues at the radio station. As far as they knew, I was just spending every day rushing around doing interviews. Soon afterwards, my programme was chosen by listeners as one of their three favourite programmes in the very first radio listeners' poll. This gave me a very good excuse to sneak off work and go and look after Little Snow in the orphanage.

Six months passed in this way, and soon it would be Little Snow's first birthday. I talked to the two women about it and we decided to have a joint celebration of the Western and Chinese New Years and birthdays for all the children and Panpan together. We would buy them new clothes, get some new toys and then I would hire a taxi and take all the children, the three adults and my *a-yi* and go into town to show them the sights and the crowds which they had never had the chance to see before.

We had it all planned, when I was sent off to do a story on child miners a day's drive away. I would be gone about two weeks and there were very few phone connections and no mobile phones at all at the time.

The night of my return home, I woke up my sleeping Panpan. He murmured 'Mama' and went back to sleep again. He was lucky, he was too small to miss people the way grown-ups do. Then my mind went back to those child miners whom I had just got to know. When would Chinese children be able to live in comfortably off, happy and loving families? I thought of Little Snow, who had absolutely nothing, and began to feel worried. I could not wait to see her sweet little rosy cheeks again . . . I thought that night would never be over.

I had the next day off and did not need to go to the radio station, so I took Panpan to see Little Snow. But the orphanage room held only the new cots – all empty.

Mother Tang was not there, and all I could make out from the assistant, who had a thick Guizhou* accent, was that the children

---

* Province in south-west China. (*Trans.*)

had been taken away. At first I thought they had been taken for a check-up, or that local government officials were looking after them for the day, but then it grew dark and began to snow heavily, and the children still had not come back. The assistant kept saying, 'I told you, the children have all been taken away!'

'Taken away where?' I was frantic but she would not say any more. She did not know where Mother Tang had gone either.

I was afraid that Panpan, who was lying asleep on a cot, might catch cold, so I went back home. When my *a-yi* heard the news, she was as worried as I was.

Over the next two weeks, I hunted frantically through the orphanage system for Mother Tang, and contacted any government departments that might know what had happened. The upshot was this: four days after I left, Mother Tang had broken her leg and had to go to hospital. She had been told nothing about what had happened to the orphanage in her absence. A young woman fresh out of university had been sent as a temporary replacement but two days later, an official turned up to say that the premises were to be demolished within a couple of weeks to make way for a national highway which had to be completed by the spring. That was the way the Chinese did things – without any legal procedures and as fast as someone could give the order! So the children were redistributed among other orphanages.

'Was each child given a number before they went?' I asked the official who claimed to be in charge.

He looked at me in surprise. 'What would we do that for? No, they weren't. Maybe the new orphanages will give them a number.'

'Are there files on each child?'

He looked even more taken aback. 'What files? No, there aren't. Maybe in their new places.'

'Then how will they ever be able to trace their birth families in the future?' I burst out.

He laughed at me: 'You must be joking! No orphans ever find their mothers!'

And that was all the answer I got.

When I next went back to the orphanage, even the new cots had been taken away. Only the assistant, who had no home to go back to, was left awaiting her fate.

'Who's taken the cots?'

'I don't know,' she said, looking panic-stricken.

'You didn't look at their documents, just let them take them away?'

'What documents? They seemed like important cadres, they were very fierce.' She looked even more frightened, and her voice trembled.

I suddenly realised that, to this illiterate country woman, there was no difference between marauding bandits and petty government officials who behaved like bandits, so I spoke more gently and stopped trying to get information out of her.

In darkened corners of the empty room, a few bits of toys lay scattered like abandoned orphans themselves.

*

Where are you, Little Snow? If only . . . I had not gone off on that assignment. That's a regret I shall carry with me always, much heavier than any stone. I never stopped making enquiries until finally, in 1996, I learned that all the orphans of Little Snow's age from that region had been adopted. I was then told that Little Snow was very likely adopted when the first group of Americans came to China. Many children from the area had been moved away and were then adopted overseas; although it was also possible, but unlikely, being a girl, that she had been adopted by a Chinese family.

As the years went by and I travelled around, I could not help looking for Little Snow, the girl with the teardrop birthmark on her forehead, my little daughter. In 2005, I went to the annual get-together of the UK-based organisation, Children Adopted From China (CACH). As I looked at more than a hundred little Chinese girls, I could not help myself: Little Snow's features seemed to be stamped on every one of those innocent, happy faces. In October 2007, I met a group of Chinese teenagers at the University of Berkeley in San Francisco, and again shed silent tears. Little Snow might have been among them, I thought. She would have been seventeen years old. I asked them to sit around me and take it in turns to read from my Mothers' Bridge of Love book. I scrutinised each face carefully, hoping to see the teardrop birthmark on one of those youthful foreheads. I did not find it, but I did not lose hope because I knew that my Little Snow would be just as pretty as they were, just as . . .

I often think that of all mothers who have lost their daughters, I am the luckiest because I can tell those young girls what their Chinese mothers really felt. And unlike their birth mothers, I can see their daughters as young women and I can embrace them in a way that they will almost certainly never be able to do.

Little Snow, my daughter, wherever you are, your mother misses you!

Afterword: Two Letters from the Heart

BEFORE I finish with my own words to all those Chinese daughters across the world, I want to bring you one more letter from an adoptive mother that encapsulates so much of what I have tried to say in this book. Nies Medema lives in Amsterdam and is the mother of two Chinese girls. This is her letter to their two different mothers, a message of gratitude and grace from one fortunate mother to two who were much less fortunate.

Dear mothers of my two daughters,

Thank you for giving birth to our daughters. We both are their mothers. I have the privilege and joy of raising them. So we are three women, with two daughters. Two mothers in China, a mother with two daughters in Amsterdam.

If one inherits character and brightness in genes you both must be bright, beautiful, smart, friendly and kindhearted. This is what I see in our daughters. They are the joy of the life of my husband and me. And missing them must cause pain in your hearts. I don't know if and how you can share this pain. I have been reading stories of Chinese mothers missing their daughters, whom they were not able to raise. I don't know what you feel, but my heart is with you.

My oldest daughter is sometimes angry with you, and sometimes she is sad. She is – as you know giving birth to her – 6.5 years old and asked me recently if you left her because you didn't love her. I tell her it's because there was no other way, because you really couldn't take care of her, and that of course you would have wanted to.

She misses you when I am sometimes angry with her. She thinks you would have been a better, more kind and friendly mother. I tell her this could be true.

But you did cause her pain, you know. Am I angry with you because you left our daughter at the gate of the train station? I believe you would have wanted to take care of her. And I am very happy you left her. This is crazy, I know, but it gave me the joy and happiness of being her mother. And she loves me too, she loves me so very much, like I love her. And yet, she would prefer to be the daughter of someone who looks more like her. She wonders about you. She wants to know, if we find you, if she has to go and live with you. I tell her she will be ours and live with us. 'But it would cause great pain to my Chinese mother if I don't come with her,' she says. I tell her it would, but that you would also be happy to see our daughter, and to see how well she is doing.

I am writing with tears in my eyes. I am very happy I am able to raise and love our daughters. It took me some time to accept myself as their 'just mother'. Did I have the right to enjoy other mothers' children? I know now I do not only have the legal right (this is just paperwork) but I do have the duty to be their 'right and true' mother, since you are not there. I cannot take your place, but I do love our daughters.

Let me tell you, my youngest daughter's mother, something funny about our child. She is light like a butterfly, her heart kind, joyful, her brain sharp, her talks witty and pleasant. We were watching cooks at work some time ago. One of them said Zuen shouldn't think of becoming a cook, because the work was very hard. She replied very self-assured: No, I will become a penguin! Another day she told us she wanted to become a peacock. In the evening she was angry she still hadn't turned into one.

So, you see, our daughters are everything a mother can hope for. We laugh, we talk, we cry, we enjoy life together. A friend asked me if I miss giving birth to them. Actually I don't. Not for myself. My daughters are mine, giving birth to them they would have been other people, and I love them like they are. I do some-times want this for my daughters, because they have to live with pain. But no one goes through life without pain. So what I do

*with them is to find ways to learn how to live with this pain. I
do hope you have found a way too.*

*We, my husband, our daughters and me, have never seen you,
but we see you in your daughter. So we love you.*

Nies Medema
(Netherlands)

*

My own message, like this book, is for their daughters, and for
daughters everywhere.

Dear daughters

I hope that by the time you have finished this book, you will
have come a little closer to finding the answer to the question
you have been asking all your lives: 'Why didn't my Chinese
mother want me?' There is no simple answer to that question.
You cannot work it out the way you do a maths sum, or find the
answer in a history book, or look it up in Xinran's books or some
academic report.

The answer lies with your birth mother. She gave you the gift
of life, and that gift, which comes with all her hopes and wishes
for you, cost her years of hardship and anguish.

Every one of us has had something we really loved in our lives.
Apart from our friends and the family, there is always something
which we have treasured and which has given us unexpected
pleasure – a perfect piece of music, a book with a story that
moves you, the boy of your dreams sitting on a park bench. These
magical moments or wonderful things leave you with intense
memories that will stay with you for ever, long after the reality
has faded or you are grown up. If such singular moments of
pleasure can stay with us for ever, imagine how much more you
meant to the mother who carried you for more than nine months
of pregnancy. She will never, ever forget you no matter why or
how you were parted from her. You, her daughter, were part of
her, bonded with her, dependent on her . . . the miracle she gave
birth to.

It may well be that your birth mother was a peasant woman

who had never left the confines of the poor mountain village where she lived and did not even know which end of a book to start reading from. Still, like the country girl in Chapter 2 or Kumei, the dish-washer girl, she will never have forgotten your wriggling movements in her belly and the pain it cost her to bring you into this world.

Then again, she may have been a lively but naïve young girl who knew nothing about life, still less about how men and women create life together. She probably did not even know when you took root in her, like 'Waiter' in Chapter 1. But she was brave enough to face social disapproval and sacrifice her own future to give you life. As you took shape in her, you gave her the strength to be a mother and understand life, and that is why, for her, memories of you will never, ever fade.

Or maybe your birth mother was a good, virtuous traditional woman who put her family first but was caught between the one-child policy and the need to produce a son to carry on the family line. Like the 'guerrilla' parents of the little girl who played 'orchid' fingers with me. They were in a terrible dilemma, yet your existence shows how they overcame their fear. If they had not protected you, you would not even have had a name, and your life would have been over in moments. Without them, you would not enjoy the sunshine, the flowers, school friends and family that you do today.

Or perhaps your birth mother is tormented by her conscience every day, and condemned by her friends and family as cold-hearted, like Green Mary. Yet the fact that she dug into that bottomless pit of pain in her heart, and put your future happiness above everything, is actually the very reason why today you can enjoy life in your adopted family and have the opportunity of living in a society where two different cultures come together.

Maybe she paid for giving birth to you with her life, as Little Snow's mother did. But I believe she has never left you; she just became part of the mountains and the seas, of the wind that caresses your face, helping you feel the changes in the seasons. She brings you peace with the night-time moonlight, and the rich textures and colours of life in the sunlight by day.

So, dear children, that you are alive and thriving today is because your mother challenged social conventions, oppression and ignorance to give you that gift of life. Valuing your own life now is a way of paying her back; fulfilling yourself is a way of thanking her.

I wrote a simple poem for Little Snow. I have written her many poems in my heart, but have never been able to send them to her. When I first went to see the film *Titanic*, for some strange reason the lines of the Céline Dion theme song, 'You're here in my heart/ And my heart will go on and on' had me rooted to my seat long after everyone had left the cinema. Somehow, through those lyrics, all my longing for little Little Snow reawakened and poured out of me.

If you want to know how I felt at that moment, just play the Céline Dion song and then read the poem below. I have put all my feelings into these words and I believe with all my heart that each mother I spoke to and whose story I have told would echo these feelings and send out her message with me:

> Beloved Child
> Do you see me in your dreams?
> Every day I wait for you . . .
> I wait
> For the wind to bring me your breath
> For the light to bring me your colours
> I pray
> The daytime makes you smile
> The night-time brings you peace
>
> Beloved Child
> If the rain touches you, it is my tears
> If the wind caresses you, it is my hand
> The daylight is my watching eye over you
> The night-time is my cradling of your dreams.
>
> Beloved Child
> Do you see me in your dreams?
> Every door that opens is my arms embracing you

Thank you
My daughter
Thank you
For being my unforgotten daughter.

Appendix A: More Letters from Adoptive Mothers

Dear Xinran

Thank you for your message. I'm sorry to burden you with this issue, especially when you are just getting over jetlag. I just thought you should know about this website and blog.

I really do think a book about birth mothers would be very important for adoptive families and also for the birth mothers who talked with you. Adoptive families need to know that it was difficult for many birth mothers to give up their children. It may be a painful story but it is part of our daughters' history nonetheless.

Although I am a Ming dynasty history specialist by training, I have tried to give my own two daughters some sense of their beginnings in China through some short stories I have written for them. I am sending them to you by attachment. Of the four stories, 'Chunyi and the Nai-nais' was published by an adoption newsletter, and I gave the publication rights to Somewhere in China a Mother Remembers (*http://www.agiftfromchina.com/webshop/shopindex.html*) to The Good Rock Foundation (http://www.goodrock.org.uk/) to support their charitable initiatives in China.

If you ever decide to publish your birth mother interviews, I would like to volunteer to help with the book.

Sincerely,
Anita M. Andrew
(Associate Professor of History,
Northern Illinois University)

*

Dear Xinran

Do you remember? We met at the Tandjung Sari Hotel in Sanur on the beachfront.

Xinran, I am so sorry we had to rush off like we did, I would have LOVED to have talked to you longer but my friends didn't want to come to Sanur in the first place as it was, as we only had 4 days in Bali.

It was my idea and really, fate just brought us there. Like I explained to you, the night before, I had opened the issue of Hello Bali *and my fingers opened the book to your exact ad; I read that, shut the book, explained how upset I was that I couldn't be in Bali on the 30th to hear you speak and the girls I travelled with were sick of me whingeing how I was going to miss you.*

Well, as I explained to you, the next day I had a whim to travel to Sanur to walk along the beachfront and suggested to the girls that we would 'just walk' until we found a nice spot and voila, the rest is history as they say.

Trouble is, Xinran, after we hurried off, I immediately regretted it and said to the girls later, I should have stayed and sent them back to Legian to finish their shopping. That night I could not sleep as I felt it was not just coincidence that led me to you. I tried to ring the next day (I hope you don't mind) but you were not around; the man at the desk said he would leave a message for you to call me but perhaps you didn't receive it (or maybe you thought 'crazy woman, she's stalking me' . . . hahahaha).

Anyway, Dear Xinran, when I got home and recounted the story of our meeting, my husband said I must fly back to Bali to meet with you again and attend your talk on the 30th. When I looked into it though, I noticed that it is the first day back at school for my children and I can't miss that.

I told him that you were writing a book with stories from Mothers who have given up their babies and he suggested that maybe our purpose in meeting was for me to compile stories from Mothers who have adopted and have you translate them and publish a book for Chinese women to read about how loved and cherished their babies are etc. . . .

I don't know what, but I do feel there was a purpose in our meeting (kind of like when you found Singyi in Wuxi in the hotel after her waiting 45 years for her lover Gu Da).

If nothing else, Xinran, I have posted about your work [with] Mothers' Bridge to our Australian Support Group and have asked people to please read your website and donate money to your cause, this at least has to be a good thing to have come out of our chance meeting.

Xinran, when are you coming to Australia and are you doing similar talks around the country? If you ever come to Darwin, we would like to extend an invitation to your husband and yourself to stay with us. We have a huge Chinese population in Darwin and I'm sure the Chung Wah society would also welcome you here (maybe that was our purpose??).

My daughter and I were talking about you last night in bed and she was giggling and getting all excited about China and being Chinese (which is good as she had been going through a funny stage of being anti-Chinese) hence why she also didn't want to go to you to be held.

She is the most wonderful child in the world and I could not love her any more if she were born to me, I know it's a terrible thing to say, but I think I even love her more than my six birth boys, perhaps that is because she is the only girl but we are as one and even at 4 yrs of age, she is my little rock and best friend.

I am forever in debt to China and her birth mother for giving me this precious gift and if I have but one wish, it would be to let her birth mother know how loved she is and how she will have every opportunity in life to prosper as she wishes.

Dear Xinran, I must go as my time on the computer is over, our new house has just been completed and we have no home line or internet access as yet. I am dependent on the public library at the moment and so can only check my emails every couple of days.

Good Luck with your talk in Ubud, I am very sad to miss it, you will be wonderful I'm sure,

Warm regards,

Kim Reinke

(Australia)

*

Hi Xinran,

I am the adoptive Mom to a precious 7 year old daughter, the love of my life, from China.

My husband and I are waiting for the referral of our second daughter which we hope will be by the end of the year.

I read your article in China Connection. Messages from Birth Mothers In China, I like that title.

I am a firm believer in the love my daughter's birth mom had for her. Please write the book.

I am the self-published author of a children's book called Letter Of Love From China, written from the birth mom's perspective to her birth daughter explaining her love for her, reasons for her relinquishment, her love for China's beauty and prayers that her child finds an adoptive family who will love her as she does.

My illustrator did a wonderful job. The illustrations are beautiful!

My book has done very well but I do get some adoptive parents who dislike the book because they prefer to tell their children they don't know if they were loved or they were 'unwanted'.

I believe if you write this book it would help families to think logically about relinquishment.

Please visit my website. Plum Blossom Books, <u>http://www.plum blossombooks.com</u>, I would be happy to send you a copy of my book.

Look forward to hearing from you.
Best Wishes,
Bonnie Cuzzolino
(USA)

Appendix B: Chinese Adoption Laws

Reform of the Adoption Law of the People's Republic of China*
Passed on 29 December 1991 at the 23rd Meeting of the Standing Committee of the Seventh National People's Congress and revised according to the Decision on the Reform of the Adoption Law of The People's Republic of China taken at the 5th Meeting of the Standing Committee of the Ninth National People's Congress on 4 November 1998.

Contents
Chapter I General Provisions
Chapter II The Establishment of Adoptive Relationship
Chapter III Validity of Adoption
Chapter IV Termination of the Adoptive Relationship
Chapter V Legal Responsibility
Chapter VI Supplementary Provisions

CHAPTER I GENERAL PROVISIONS
Article 1—This Law is enacted to protect the lawful adoptive relationship and to safeguard the rights of parties involved in the adoptive relationship.
Article 2—Adoption shall be in the interest of the upbringing and growth of adopted minors and in the protection of the legitimate rights of the adoptee and the adopter, in conformity with the principle of equality and voluntariness, and not in contravention of social morality.

---

* Sourced from the official CCAA website. (*Trans.*)

Article 3—Adoption shall not contravene laws and regulations on family planning.

CHAPTER II THE ESTABLISHMENT OF ADOPTIVE RELATIONSHIP

Article 4—Minors under the age of 14, as enumerated below, may be adopted.

(1) orphans bereaved of parents;
(2) abandoned infants or children whose parents cannot be ascertained or found; or
(3) children whose parents are unable to rear them due to unusual difficulties.

Article 5—The following citizens or institutions are entitled to place out children for adoption:

(1) guardians of an orphan;
(2) social welfare institutions;
(3) parents unable to rear their children due to unusual difficulties.

Article 6—Adopters shall meet simultaneously the following requirements:

(1) childless;
(2) capable of rearing and educating the adoptee;
(3) no illness which is deemed medically as inappropriate for the adopter to adopt children; and
(4) having reached the age of 30.

Article 7—The adoption of a child belonging to a collateral relative by blood of the same generation and up to the third degree of kinship, may not be confined to the restrictions specified in Item (3), Article 4; Item (3), Article 5; and Article 9 of this law as well as the restriction of a minor under the age of 14.

An overseas Chinese, in adopting a child belonging to a collateral relative by blood of the same generation and up to the third degree of kinship, may also be not subject to the adopter childless status.

Article 8—The adopter may adopt one child only, male or female.

Orphans, disabled children or abandoned infants and children, who are raised in the social welfare institutes, and whose biological parents cannot be ascertained or found, may be adopted irrespective of the restrictions that the adopter shall be childless and adopt one child only.

Article 9—Where a male person without spouse adopts a female child, the age difference between the adopter and adoptee shall be no less than 40 years.

Article 10—Where the parents intend to place out their child for adoption, they must act in concert. If one parent cannot be ascertained or found, the other parent may place out the child for adoption alone.

Where a person with spouse adopts a child, the husband and wife must adopt the child in concert.

Article 11—Adoption of a child and the placing out of the child for the adoption shall both take place on a voluntary basis. Where the adoption involves a minor aged 10 or more, the consent of the adoptee shall be obtained.

Article 12—If the parents of a minor are both persons without full civil capacity, the guardian(s) of the minor may not place out him (her) for adoption, except when the parents may do serious harm to the minor.

Article 13—Where a guardian intends to place out an orphaned minor for adoption, the guardian must obtain the consent of the person who has obligations to support the orphan. Where the person who has obligations to support the orphan disagrees to have the orphan adopted, and the guardian is unwilling to continue the performance of his guardianship, it is necessary to change the guardian in accordance with the General Principles of the Civil Law of the People's Republic of China.

Article 14—A step-father or step-mother may, with the consent of the parents of the step-son or step-daughter, adopt the step-son or step-daughter, and such adoption may be free from the restrictions specified in Item (3), Article 4; Item (3), Article 5 and Article 6 of this law, as well as from the restriction that the adoptee must be under the age of 14 and the adopter may adopt one child only.

Article 15—Adoption shall be registered at the department of civil affairs of the people's government above county level. The adoptive relationship comes into force on the date of its registration.

The department of civil affairs in charge of registration shall, prior to the registration, make an announcement in the adoption of abandoned infants and children whose biological parents cannot be ascertained or found.

Should the parties involved in the adoptive relationship wish to conclude an adoption agreement, a written agreement on adoption shall be concluded.

Should the parties or one of the parties involved in the adoptive relationship wish that the adoption be notarized, the adoption shall be notarized.

Article 16—After the establishment of adoptive relationship, the public security organ shall, in accordance with the relevant rules and regulations of the State, carry out registration of residence for the adoptee.

Article 17—Orphans or children whose parents are unable to rear them may be supported by relatives or friends of their parents.

The adoptive relationship shall not apply to the relationship between the supporter and the supported.

Article 18—Where a spouse places out a minor child for adoption after the death of the other spouse, the parents of the deceased shall have the priority in rearing the child.

Article 19—The parents of a child adopted by others may not bear any more child[ren] in violation of the regulations on family planning on the ground of having placed out their child for adoption.

Article 20—It is strictly forbidden to buy or sell a child or to do so under the cloak of adoption.

Article 21—A foreigner may, in accordance with this law, adopt a child (male or female) in the People's Republic of China.

When a foreigner adopts a child in the People's Republic of China, his or her adoption shall be examined and approved by the responsible agency of the adopter's resident country in accordance with the country's law. The adopter shall submit papers certifying such particulars of the adopter as age, marital status, profession, property, health, and whether subjected once to criminal punishment, which are provided by the authoritative agency of his or her resident country. Such certifying papers shall be authenticated by the department of foreign affairs of the country of his or her residence, [or the] agency authorised by the department of foreign affairs and by the Embassy or Consulate of the People's Republic of China in the country concerned. The adopter shall conclude a written agreement with the person placing out the child for adoption and register in person with the department of civil affairs of the people's government at the provincial level.

Should the parties or one of the parties involved in the adoptive relationship request to carry out notarization, they shall go to a designated notary agency qualified for foreign-related notarization authorised by the judicial administration department of the State Council for adoptive notarization.

Article 22—When the adopter and the person placing out the child for adoption wish to make a secret of the adoption, others shall respect their wish and shall not make a disclosure thereof.

CHAPTER III VALIDITY OF ADOPTION

Article 23—As of the date of establishment of the adoptive relationship, the legal provisions governing the relationship between parents and children shall apply to the rights and duties in the relationship between adoptive parents and adopted children; the legal provisions governing the relationship between children and close relatives of their parents shall apply to the rights and duties in the relationship between adopted children and close relatives of the adoptive parents.

The rights and duties in the relationship between an adopted child and his or her parents and other close relatives shall terminate with the establishment of the adoptive relationship.

Article 24—An adopted child may adopt his or her adoptive father's or adoptive mother's surname, and may also retain his or her original surname, if so agreed through consultation between the parents concerned.

Article 25—Any act of adoption contravening the provisions of Article 55 of the General Principles of the Civil Law of the People's Republic of China and those of this law shall be of no legal validity.

Any act of adoption ruled to be invalid by a people's court shall be of no legal validity from the very start of the act.

CHAPTER IV TERMINATION OF THE ADOPTIVE RELATIONSHIP

Article 26—No adopter may terminate the adoptive relationship before the adoptee comes of age, except when the adopter and the person having placed out the child for the adoption agree to terminate such relationship. If the adopted child involved reaches the age of 10 or more, his or her consent shall be obtained.

Where an adopter fails to perform the duty of rearing the adoptee or commits maltreatment, abandonment, or other acts of encroachment upon the lawful rights of the minor adopted child, the person having placed out the child for adoption has the right to demand the termination of the adoptive relationship. Where the adopter and the person having placed out the child for adoption fail to reach an agreement thereon, a suit may be brought in a people's court.

Article 27—Where the relationship between the adoptive parents and an adult adopted child deteriorates to such a degree that their living together in the same household becomes impossible, they may terminate their adoptive relationship by agreement. In the absence of an agreement, they may bring a suit in a people's court.

Article 28—When reaching an agreement on the termination of the adoptive relationship, the parties involved shall complete the procedure for registering the termination of the adoptive relationship at a department of civil affairs.

Article 29—Upon the termination of an adoptive relationship, the rights and duties in the relationship between an adopted child and his or her adoptive parents and their close relatives shall also terminate, and the rights and duties in the relationship between the child and his or her parents and their close relatives shall be restored automatically. However, with respect to the rights and duties in the relationship between an adult adopted child and his or her parents and their close relatives, it may be decided through consultation as to whether to restore them.

Article 30—Upon termination of an adoptive relationship, an adult adopted child who has been reared by the adoptive parents shall provide an amount of money to support the adoptive parents who have lost ability to work and are short of any source of income. If the adoptive relationship is terminated on account of the maltreatment or desertion of the adoptive parents by the grown-up adopted child, the adoptive parents may demand a compensation from the adopted child for the living and education expenses paid during the period of adoption.

If the parents of an adopted child request the termination of the adoptive relationship, the adoptive parents may demand an appropriate compensation from the parents for the living and education expenses paid during the period of adoption, except if the adoptive relationship is terminated on account of the maltreatment or desertion of the adoption of the adopted child by the adoptive parents.

CHAPTER V LEGAL RESPONSIBILITY

Article 31—Whoever abducts and traffics in a child under the cloak of adoption shall be investigated for criminal responsibility in accordance with [the] law.

Whoever abandons an infant shall be fine[d] by the public security organ; if the circumstances constitute a crime, the offender shall be investigated for criminal responsibility in accordance with [the] law.

Whoever buys or sells children shall have the illegal proceeds confiscated by the public security organ, and shall be fined. If the circumstances constitute a crime, the offender shall be investigated for criminal responsibility in accordance with [the] law.

CHAPTER VI SUPPLEMENTARY PROVISIONS

Article 32—The people's congress and its standing committee in a national autonomous area may, on the basis of the principles of this Law and in the light of the local conditions, formulate adaptive or supplementary provisions. The relevant regulations of a national autonomous region shall be submitted to the Standing Committee of the National People's Congress for the record. The relevant regulations of an autonomous prefecture or autonomous county shall be submitted to the standing committee of the provincial or autonomous region's people's congress for approval before coming into force, and shall also be submitted to the Standing Committee of the National People's Congress for the record.

Article 33—The State Council may, in accordance with this law, formulate measures for its implementation.

Article 34—This Law shall enter into force on April 1, 1992.

*

Population and Family Planning Law of the People's Republic of China*
Adopted at the 25th Meeting of the Standing Committee of the Ninth National People's Congress on 29 December 2001.

Contents
Chapter I General Provisions
Chapter II Formulation and Implementation of Population
    Development Plans
Chapter III Regulation of Reproduction
Chapter IV Rewards and Social Security

---

* From the Chinese government law website http://www.gov.cn/english/laws/2005-10/11/content_75954.htm. (*Trans.*)

CHAPTER I GENERAL PROVISIONS

Article 1—This Law is enacted, in accordance with the Constitution, for the purpose of bringing about a coordinated development between population on the one side and the economy, society, resources and environment on the other, promoting family planning, protecting the legitimate rights and interests of citizens, enhancing happiness of fam-ilies, and contributing to prosperity of the nation and progress of the society.

Article 2—China being a populous country, family planning is a fundamental State policy.

The State adopts a comprehensive measure to control the size and raise the general quality of the population.

The State relies on publicity and education, advances in science and technology, multi-purpose services and the establishment and improvement of the reward and social security systems in carrying out the population and family planning programs.

Article 3—The population and family planning programs shall be combined with the efforts to offer more opportunities for women to receive education and get employed, improve their health and elevate their status.

Article 4—When promoting family planning, the people's governments at all levels and their staff members shall perform their administrative duties strictly in accordance with [the] law, and enforce the law in a civil manner, and they may not infringe upon legitimate rights and interests of citizens.

Lawful performance of the official duties by the administrative departments for family planning and their staff members shall be protected by [the] law.

Article 5—The State Council shall exercise leadership over the population and family planning programs throughout the country. Local people's governments at all levels shall exercise leadership over the population and family planning programs within their own administrative regions.

Article 6—The administrative department for family planning under the State Council shall be in charge of the family planning program and the population program related to family planning nationwide.

Family planning administration departments of the local people's governments at or above the county level shall be in charge of the family planning program and the population program related to family planning within their own administrative regions.

The other administrative departments of the local people's governments at or above the county level shall be in charge of the relevant aspects of the population and family planning programs within the limits of their duties.

Article 7—Public organizations such as Trade Unions, Communist Youth Leagues, Women's Federations, and Family Planning Associations, as well as enterprises, institutions, and individual citizens shall assist the people's governments in carrying out the population and family planning programs.

Article 8—The State gives rewards to organizations and individuals that have scored outstanding achievements in the population program and family planning.

CHAPTER II FORMULATION AND IMPLEMENTATION OF POPULATION DEVELOP-
MENT PLANS

Article 9—The State Council shall make plans for population development and incorporate them into the national economic and social development plans. Based on the plans for population development nationwide and such plans made by the people's governments at the next higher level, people's governments at or above the county level shall, in light of their local conditions, work out such plans for their own administrative regions and incorporate them into their economic and social development plans.

Article 10—People's governments at or above the county level shall, on the basis of the population development plans, formulate plans for implementation of the population and family planning programs and make arrangements for their implementation.

The administrative departments for family planning of the people's governments at or above the county level shall be responsible for routine implementation of the population and family planning plans.

People's governments of townships, ethnic townships, and towns, and neighborhood offices in urban areas shall be in charge of the population and family planning programs in the areas under their jurisdiction and shall implement the population and family planning plans.

Article 11—In the implementation plans for population and family planning programs shall be specified measures for keeping the size of the population under control, improving maternal and child healthcare services, and raising the general quality of the population.

Article 12—Villagers' committees and residents' committees shall, in accordance with [the] law, make a success of the family planning programs. Government departments, the armed forces, public organizations, enterprises and institutions shall make a success of the family planning programs in their own units.

Article 13—Departments in charge of family planning, education, science and technology, culture, public health, civil affairs, the press and publication, and radio and television broadcasting shall make arrangements to conduct public education in the importance of the population program and family planning. The mass media are obligated to give publicity to the population program and family planning for the public good.

Schools shall, in a manner suited to the characteristics of the receivers and in a planned way, conduct among pupils education in physiology and health, puberty or sexual health.

Article 14—Family planning among migrant people shall jointly be managed by the people's governments of the place where their residence is registered and of the place where they are currently staying, but chiefly by the latter.

Article 15—The State, on the basis of the national economic and social development, gradually increases the overall amount of funding for the population and family planning programs. People's governments at all levels shall guarantee the necessary funding for the said programs.

People's governments at all levels shall give special support to the population and family planning programs in poverty-stricken areas and in areas inhabited by ethnic [minority] peoples.

The State encourages public organizations, enterprises and institutions and individuals to offer financial assistance to the population and family planning programs.

No unit or individual may withhold, reduce or misappropriate the funds earmarked for the population and family planning programs.

Article 16—The State encourages scientific research and international exchange and cooperation in respect of the population and family planning programs.

CHAPTER III REGULATION OF REPRODUCTION

Article 17—Citizens have the right to reproduction as well as the obligation to practice family planning according to [the] law. Both husband and wife bear equal responsibility for family planning.

Article 18—The State maintains its current policy for reproduction, encouraging late marriage and childbearing and advocating one child per couple. Where the requirements specified by laws and regulations are met, plans for a second child, if requested, may be made. Specific measures in this regard shall be formulated by the People's Congress or its standing committee of a province, autonomous region, or municipality directly under the Central Government.

Family planning shall also be introduced to the ethnic [minority] peoples. Specific measures in this regard shall be formulated by the People's Congress or its standing committee of a province, autonomous region, or municipality directly under the Central Government.

Article 19—Family planning shall be practiced chiefly by means of contraception.

The State creates conditions to ensure that individual citizens knowingly choose safe, effective, and appropriate contraceptive methods. Where birth control operations are performed, the recipients' safety shall be ensured.

Article 20—Couples of reproductive age shall conscientiously adopt contraceptive methods and accept technical services and guidance for family planning.

Incidence of unwanted pregnancies shall be prevented and reduced.

Article 21—Couples of reproductive age who practice family planning shall receive, free of charge, the basic items of technical services specified by the State.

The funds needed for rendering the services specified in the preceding paragraph shall, in accordance with relevant State regulations, be listed in the budget or be guaranteed by social insurance plans.

Article 22—Discrimination against and maltreatment of women who give birth to baby girls or who suffer from infertility are prohibited. Discrimination against, maltreatment, and abandonment of baby girls are prohibited.

CHAPTER IV REWARDS AND SOCIAL SECURITY

Article 23—The State, in accordance with regulations, rewards couples who practice family planning.

Article 24—To facilitate family planning, the State establishes and improves the social security system covering the basic old-age insurance, basic medical insurance, childbearing insurance, and welfare benefits.

The State encourages insurance companies to offer insurance schemes that facilitate family planning.

In rural areas where conditions permit, various types of old-age support schemes may be adopted in adherence to the principles of government guidance and willingness on the part of the rural people.

Article 25—Citizens who marry late and delay childbearing may be entitled to longer nuptial and maternity leaves or other welfare benefits.

Article 26—In accordance with relevant State regulations, women shall enjoy special occupational protection and be entitled to assistance and subsidies during the period of pregnancy, delivery, and breast-feeding.

Citizens who undergo surgical operation for family planning shall enjoy leaves as specified by the State. Local people's governments may give them rewards.

Article 27—The State shall issue to a couple who volunteer to have only one child in their lifetime a 'Certificate of Honor for Single-Child Parents'. Couples who are issued the said certificate shall enjoy rewards in accordance with the relevant regulations of the State and of the province, autonomous region, or municipality directly under the Central Government.

Where measures in laws, rules or regulations specify that the rewards to couples who have only one child in their lifetime shall be given by the units where they work, such units shall execute the measures.

Where the only child of a couple is disabled or killed in an accident, and the couple decides not to have or adopt another child, the local people's government shall provide the couple with necessary assistance.

Article 28—Local people's governments at all levels shall help rural households that practice family planning to develop economic undertakings by giving them support and preferential treatment in terms of funds, technology and training.

Poverty-stricken households that practice family planning shall be given priority in terms of poverty-alleviation loans, relief through work and other poverty-alleviation projects, and social assistance.

Article 29—Specific measures for conferring rewards specified in this Chapter may be formulated by the people's congresses or their standing committees or the people's governments of the provinces, autonomous regions, municipalities directly under the Central Government or larger cities in accordance with the provisions of this Law and relevant laws and administrative regulations and in light of local conditions.

CHAPTER V TECHNICAL SERVICES FOR FAMILY PLANNING

Article 30—The State establishes premarital health care and maternal health care systems to prevent or reduce the incidence of birth defects and improve the health of newborns.

Article 31—People's governments at all levels shall take measures to ensure citizens' access to technical services for family planning in order to improve their reproductive health.

Article 32—Local people's governments at all levels shall rationally allocate and make multi-purpose use of health resources, establish and improve family planning technical service networks comprising family planning technical service institutions and medical and healthcare institutions providing such services and upgrade the facilities and improve the conditions for and raise the level of such services.

Article 33—Family planning technical service institutions and medical and healthcare institutions providing such services shall, within the scope of their respective responsibilities, conduct, among different reproductive age groups of people, publicity and education in the basic knowledge about the population program and family planning, provide pregnancy check-ups and follow-up for married women of reproductive age, offer advice and guidance and provide technical services in respect of family planning and reproductive health.

Article 34—Persons providing family planning technical services shall give guidance to citizens who practice family planning in choosing the safe, effective and appropriate contraceptive methods.

Couples who already have children are encouraged to choose long-acting contraceptive methods.

The State encourages research in, employment and wide use of new technologies and contraceptives for family planning.

Article 35—Use of ultrasonography or other techniques to identify fetal sex for non-medical purposes is strictly prohibited. Sex-selective pregnancy termination for non-medical purposes is strictly prohibited.

CHAPTER VI LEGAL LIABILITY

Article 36—Anyone who, in violation of the provisions of this Law, commits one of the following acts shall be instructed to make rectification and be given a disciplinary warning, and his unlawful gains shall be confiscated by the administrative department for family planning or public health; if the unlawful gains exceed 10,000 yuan, he shall be fined not less than two times but not more than six times the amount of the unlawful gains; if there are no unlawful gains or the said gains are less than 10,000 yuan, he shall be fined not less than 10,000 yuan but not more than 30,000 yuan; if the circumstances are serious, his license shall be revoked by the authority that issued it; if a crime is constituted, he shall be investigated for criminal liability in accordance with [the] law:

(1) illegally performing an operation related to family planning on another person;

(2) Using ultrasonography or other techniques to identify fetal gender for non-medical purposes or to bring about sex-selective pregnancy termination for non-medical purposes for another person; or

(3) performing a fake birth-control operation, providing a false medical report, or issuing a counterfeit certificate of family planning.

Article 37—If anyone forges, alters or trades in certificates of family planning, his unlawful gains shall be confiscated by the administrative department for family planning; if the said gains exceed 5,000 yuan, he shall be fined not less than two times but not more than ten times the amount of the said gains; if there are no such gains or the gains are less than 5,000 yuan, he shall be fined not less than 5,000 yuan but not more than 20,000 yuan. If the offense constitutes a crime, he shall be investigated for criminal liability in accordance with [the] law.

A certificate of family planning that is obtained by illegitimate means shall be revoked by the administrative department for family planning; if the fault lies with the unit that issues such a certificate, the persons who are directly in charge and the other persons who are directly responsible shall be given administrative sanctions in accordance with [the] law.

Article 38—Persons providing technical services for family planning who serve against rules and regulations or delay rescue measures, diagnosis or treatment, if the consequences are serious, shall, in accordance with relevant laws and administrative regulations, bear appropriate legal liability.

Article 39—Any functionary of a State organ who commits one of the following acts in the work of family planning, if the act constitutes a crime, shall be investigated for criminal liability in accordance with [the] law; if it does not constitute a crime, he shall be given an administrative sanction in accordance with [the] law; his unlawful gains, if any, shall be confiscated:

(1) infringing on a citizen's personal rights, property rights or other legitimate rights and interests;

(2) abusing his power, neglecting his duty or engaging in malpractices for personal gain;

(3) demanding or accepting bribes;

(4) withholding, reducing, misappropriating or embezzling funds for family planning or social maintenance fees; or

(5) making false or deceptive statistical data on population or family planning, or fabricating, tampering with, or refusing to provide such data.

Article 40—Any unit that, in violation of the provisions of this Law, fails to perform its obligation of assisting in the administration of family planning shall be instructed to make rectification and be criticised in a circular by the local people's government concerned; the persons who are directly in charge and the other persons who are directly responsible shall be given administrative sanctions in accordance with [the] law.

Article 41—Citizens who give birth to babies not in compliance with the provisions of Article 18 of this Law shall pay a social maintenance fee prescribed by law.

Citizens who fail to pay the full amount of the said fees payable within the specified time limit shall have to pay an additional surcharge each in accordance with relevant State regulations, counting from the date each fails to pay the fees; with regard to ones who still fail to make the payment, the administrative department for family planning that makes the decision on collection of the fees shall, in accordance with [the] law, apply to the People's Court for enforcement.

Article 42—Where the person who should pay the social maintenance fees in accordance with the provisions prescribed in Article 41 of this Law is a State functionary, he shall, in addition, be given an administrative sanction in accordance with [the] law; with regard to a person other than the State functionary, a disciplinary measure shall, in addition, be taken against him by the unit or organization where he belongs.

Article 43—Anyone who resists or hinders the administrative department for family planning or its staff members in their performance of their official duties in accordance with [the] law shall be subject to criticism and be stopped by the administrative department for family planning. If his act constitutes a violation of the administrative regulations for public security, he shall, in accordance with [the] law, be given a penalty for the violation; if it constitutes a crime, he shall be investigated for criminal liability.

Article 44—Citizens, legal persons or other organizations that believe an administrative department infringes upon their legitimate rights and interests while administering the family planning program may, in accordance with [the] law, appeal for administrative review or initiate administrative proceedings.

CHAPTER VII SUPPLEMENTARY PROVISIONS

Article 45—Specific measures for family planning among migrant persons and for providing to them family planning technical services, and measures for collecting social maintenance fees shall be formulated by the State Council.

Article 46—Specific measures for implementing this Law by the Chinese People's Liberation Army shall be formulated by the Central Military Commission in accordance with this Law.

Article 47—This Law shall go into effect as of September 1, 2002.

Appendix C: Suicide among Women

SCIENTISTS TELL us that suicide is one of the largest causes of death among young Chinese people, with women and girls most at risk.

In an essay published in the British medical journal *The Lancet*, Chinese and US scientists say that suicide is China's fifth biggest killer, accounting for 3.6 per cent of all deaths. This investigation, based on data from the Chinese Ministry of Health from 1995 to 1999, revealed that one in every five Chinese people who died aged 15 to 34 had committed suicide. These researchers came from two well-known psychiatric hospitals: Beijing Huilong Hospital and the Harvard Medical School in Massachusetts. They said that China is one of the few countries in the world where the female suicide rate is higher than that for males: 25 per cent more women commit suicide than men.

Young peasant women

They said that what made China unique was that the differences in the rate of successful suicides originated in a very high suicide rate among young peasant women. In the 15–34 age bracket, 30 per cent of women and girls who had died were suicides; the rate among their male contemporaries was only 12.5 per cent.

The research showed that this high suicide rate among women was the consequence of attempts at self-injury. All over the world, women are more prone to self-injury than men. In China, powerful agricultural chemicals are easy to get hold of, and there is a shortage of medical personnel in rural areas. This means that virtually all suicide attempts were successful, even though the women who killed themselves did not necessarily truly wish to die.

*Elderly peasants**

The research has found that elderly people in the countryside are the group most likely to take their own lives; as a proportion of the population, their suicide rate is twice as high as that of young women. The writers of the article say that the fact that traditional Chinese culture gives old people a very high status makes this discovery particularly worthy of attention.

Research suggests that there are no strong religious or legal prohibitions against suicide in China. It also lacks a social welfare system, or other safety nets.

The research reveals that 38 per cent of suicides in China are mentally ill. That is to say, the suicide of the rest is a consequence of extreme pressure, perhaps from serious illness or money difficulties.

---

* In China before 1999, 78% of the population were peasants.

Appendix D: The 18 Wonders of Chengdu

EVERYWHERE IN China has its list of 'Wonders', and these are constantly changing. The *18 Wonders of Chengdu* below were those that were current at the end of the 1980s.

1. Chengdu people get sick if they don't go to a tea house every day.
The people of Chengdu love their tea. At that time, the population of the metropolitan district of Chengdu was over 10 million, and of the city itself, three million or more – and 200,000 of those actually spent their days in the city's tea houses. People used to say that the Beijingers went in pursuit of opportunities, the Shanghainese in pursuit of fashion; for Guangdong people it was money, but what Chengdu people wanted was to live life as it was. As they put it, earn a bit of money, go to a little tea house, play a bit of mah-jong, eat a few nice kebabs, watch a video or two, and buy a few *chacha* shares.*

2. Those clever Chengdu women are adorable.
The women of Chengdu are noted for their beauty. The reason is that the climate is very humid, as it is in all of Sichuan, so the Sichuanese eat a lot of hot pepper, which makes them sweat and gets rid of fat. Losing weight makes them more beautiful. There's a bit of doggerel which goes: 'Go to Beijing for the buildings, to Shanghai for the people, to Hainan Island for the prostitutes, to the north-east for big people, to Xi'an for the tombs, to Yunnan for the karst outcrops, and to Chengdu for the girls.' And there's another: 'In Beijing, you feel insignificant, in

---

* That is, small or worthless shares. (*Trans.*)

Guangdong you feel poor, in Hainan Island you feel ill, and in Chengdu you feel you got married too soon.'

3. Chengdu men love those beautiful women who bend their ears.
There are associations of football fans everywhere, but there's an unusual association in Chengdu, the Ear-bending Association. What does ear-bending mean? It's an association of men who go in fear of their wives who bend their ears until they obey orders.

4. Chengdu people eat pickles at every meal.
Chengdu people are methodical in their eating habits. The three key elements of their diet are pickled vegetables, hotpot and tea. They need hotpot to nourish them, the tea cuts the excess grease, and the pickles, apart from being a way of eating vegetables, aid the digestion. Pickles and hotpot make an ideal combination. As the saying goes, 'If you put meat and vegetables together, the rice doesn't get wasted; if you put men and women together, they don't get tired.'

5. Vendors of 'gamblers' snacks' shout their wares every night.
Chengdu people love to stay up playing mah-jong, and the young love to run around all night. By midnight they're hungry, and are looking for 'gamblers' snacks'. Most restaurants shut early, so night-time food is sold by street vendors off the back of their tricycles. Some of them make a living out of this, and a very good one too, because their customers are all card-players and gamblers. If it's a winning gambler who's paying up, they're not going to bother about the price they pay, and if it's the loser paying, then it's worth them eating to make up a bit for having lost.

6. There are mah-jong games on every street corner.
Chengdu is a leisurely city, and its inhabitants spend their time drinking tea, going out to eat and playing mah-jong. People will take any opportunity to play mah-jong: they play at family celebrations, they play at funerals, they play on weekend trips to village restaurants, they go home from work, have dinner and play mah-jong. Everybody does it all the time. Some men gamble until the wives leave and take their children with them, but gamblers can't leave their beloved game.

7. When a mouse dies, everyone gathers around to look.
Chengdu people love a bit of scandal in the street. As the saying goes, 'You only have to spit to get three circles of people around you.' If you don't believe me, try it out: if you see an ant moving house in the street, watch it very carefully. Probably someone will come up and ask you what you're looking at. When you tell her, she won't believe you, so she'll squat down with you and have a good look. Once you've got two or three people looking, within half an hour you'll have at least a dozen onlookers.

8. Everyone rushes to sunbathe every time the sun comes out.
Chengdu has strange weather. 'Sichuan dogs bark at the sun,' as they say, because the sun is such a rarity there. If the sun shines in winter, then everyone and their friends rush off to the country for a meal in a village restaurant or make for the nearest tea house to bask in a patch of sunlight. Chengdu people say that sunning oneself in winter gets rid of damp in the body.

9. No one can beat the people of Chengdu at gossiping and bragging.
People all over China do it, and have different words for it, but in Chengdu they're the best.

10. In Chengdu, guests get treated to a foot or a head massage.
Chengdu people enjoy entertaining. If they want to make friends with you or have something they want your help with, first they'll invite you for a big meal. When you've eaten and drunk your fill, then they'll take you to a massage salon for a relaxing foot or head massage.

11. Small traders have the most carefree life.
That means small traders who spend their days sitting in tea houses, listening to Sichuan opera, legs crossed and knees jiggling in time to the music. They have no pressures on them and no responsibilities, and don't care about appearances. People may look down on them as mean-spirited. But they know quite well that they have the most carefree lives.

12. Even successful business people love their fly-blown cafés.
Chengdu has a lot of people who have made it big in business, but in

spite of their money, the thing they really love is to while away the hours in a noisy tea house or a fly-blown café, or pick up a couple of kebabs or some other snack from a little street stand.

13. People set up their chess games on every street corner.
You can see chess players in every main street and back alley. On the main streets, you don't necessarily get the chess champions, but you'll never beat them. The best you can hope for is a draw, but that way you'll never win any money.

14. Chengdu young misses turn into young madams.
If you see an old lady in Chengdu, you should address her as Big Sister; a younger woman, you should call Little Sister; and a middle-aged mum got up like a young woman, you should call her Little Sister too.

15. All the women wear leather shoes.
Smart Chengdu women used to wear brand-name clothes and gold rings on their fingers. Then later, imported luxury furniture became the mark of smartness. Women who don't have the money to buy real leather shoes wear imitation leather shoes.

16. The more newspapers there are, the better they sell.
Everyone in Chengdu likes reading the newspaper. It's the first thing they do when they go to the tea house, and sometimes they read the most amazing things in them. Then they get on the phone and tell their friends about it. Chengdu's newspapers support a large number of journalists and writers. The number of newspapers also brings them all together in one place and gives Chengdu a very cultured atmosphere.

17. Bicycles come with umbrellas over the seat.
In Chengdu, rain comes from the east as the sun sets in the west. In the evening, the sun blazes out in the west as it goes down behind the mountain. Chengdu women often get an umbrella stand fixed to the back of the bicycle, and stick their umbrella on it.

18. It's quicker to go to work by bicycle than by bus.
Chengdu has many names, like turtle city and brocade city, but it has

another name too: its residents call it traffic-jam city. So Chengdu is the kingdom of the bicycle – almost every resident has one, and bicycle shops do a roaring trade.

Acknowledgements

M Y HEARTFELT THANKS:

To the Chinese mothers who have talked to me from the bottom of their hearts and told me about their secret lives; to the Chinese daughters who have asked me about their roots and have trusted me; to the Western adoptive families who have written to me and encouraged me to be brave and represent the secret Chinese mothers to their beloved daughters from China . . . My soul has been watered again and again by my tears as I wrote this book and felt your pain and your love.

To Nicky Harman my translator, Alison Samuel my editor, all the people who work at Toby Eady Associates, and to everyone who has worked on this book: together you have helped me to make those secret Chinese mothers known in English, and helped me to share their love for their daughters with readers all over the world . . .

The Mothers' Bridge of Love charity has formed a bridge between different cultures, and brought together countless volunteers of all ages, from the over-fifties down to pre-school children, from a score or more countries, all of them in search of Chinese culture. Together we have undertaken the task of helping adopted children to find their Chinese roots. Together we have shared the happiness of thousands of adoptive families whom we have involved in our activities. We have felt our way painfully across the gulf that divides Western and Chinese cultures; we have been inspired by the support that children have found in The Mothers' Bridge of Love. Every single volunteer has become an indispensable part of The Mothers' Bridge of Love activities. As for the following, I believe their contribution to building bridges between cultures is beyond price: MBL former CEO Meiyee Lim and Wendy Wu; MBL trustees Emily Buchanan, Toby Eady, Jeremy Gordon, Ching-He Huang, Christina Lamb, Kailan Xue; MBL team leaders and every single MBL volunteer in many different countries, as well as MBL's legal adviser Wilfrid Vernor-Miles. Forgive me for not naming all of you volunteers individually, and please accept my heartfelt thanks for your enthusiasm for Chinese culture, and the loving work you have done for Chinese children and their mothers. My gratitude to you all is boundless.

www.mothersbridge.org

Support MBL—'The Mothers' Bridge of Love' for Chinese Children

Since the publication of *The Good Women of China* and the books which followed, Xinran has received numerous letters from women all over the world – some from adoptive mothers of Chinese children, some from overseas Chinese mothers. All of them were concerned with such issues as those raised in the questions given below. As a result, she decided to create a charity – The Mothers' Bridge of Love (MBL) – to help these women and their children, as well as the many children living in destitute conditions in China.

More than 120,000 Western families have adopted Chinese orphans, mainly girls, since 1993. As they grow up, this is one of the first questions those children might ask: 'Why didn't my Chinese mummy want me?'

With over 50 per cent of the Chinese people living in poverty, millions of children all around the country can only dream of a decent education: 'How can I ever go to school?'

Meanwhile, millions of overseas Chinese children hardly understand their roots: 'What is Chinese culture?'

The Mothers' Bridge of Love helps to find answers to these questions by building a bridge:
– between China and the rest of the world;
– between rich and poor;
– between birth culture and adoptive culture.

If these questions pull at your heartstrings, please support MBL by sending a donation.

Please POST your cheque to:
MBL
9 ORME COURT
LONDON W2 4RL
UK

Please WIRE money to:
The Mothers Bridge of Love (MBL)
Sort Code: 400607
Account Number: 11453130

HSBC Bank
Russell Square Branch
1 Woburn Place, Russell Square
London WC1H 0LQ
SWIFT Code: MIDL GB2142E

Your support will improve the lives of Chinese children from country to country, village to village and girl to girl.